Recess

Rediscovering Play and Purpose

Laurie Haller

Cass Community Publishing House

an imprint of
David Crumm Media, LLC
Canton, Michigan

For more information and further discussion, visit
www.lauriehaller.org

To order the book, visit
www.ccpublishinghouse.org

The Holy Bible, King James Version. Cambridge Edition: 1769. Used with permission.

Cover art and design by
Rick Nease
www.RickNeaseArt.com

Published By
The Cass Community Publishing House
an imprint of
David Crumm Media, LLC
42015 Ford Rd., Suite 234
Canton, Michigan, USA

For information about customized editions, bulk purchases or permissions, contact Cass Community Publishing House at ccumcac@aol.com.

Contents

Acknowledgments vii

Praise for *Recess: Rediscovering Play and Purpose* ix

Preface xv

Introduction xix

Disengagement 2

Floundering 18

Transition 41

Freedom 57

Seeing and Listening 73

Wasting Time With Jesus 98

Playing 122

Transformation 141

On the Road 159

Darkness and Light 174

Recess 194

Preparation 204

Re-Entry 212

Epilogue 227

Report to the Clergy in the
West Michigan Annual Conference 232

About the Author 238

Dedicated to my parents, Gwen and Gerry Hartzel, who first taught me about God's love and modeled a life of faith that has shaped who I am today.

Acknowledgments

THIS BOOK WOULD not have been completed without the unfailing support of my husband, Gary, my beloved, who has been a constant source of encouragement as well as my partner in ministry. Our children, Sarah, Garth and Talitha, have taught me how important recess is by their courageous spirits and love of adventure, play and the journey itself.

I give thanks for the laity in the churches I have served over the years, for they are the ones who molded and formed my vocation: Stratford United Methodist Church (Stratford, Connecticut) and congregations in Michigan: Ogdensburg United Methodist Church; Hart United Methodist Church; First United Methodist Church, Grand Rapids; Aldersgate and Plainfield United Methodist Churches, Grand Rapids; First United Methodist Church, Birmingham. I am especially indebted to many mentors in the community of faith where I was raised, Zion Mennonite Church in Souderton, Pennsylvania.

Several special friends have been an important part of my spiritual journey during and after the writing of this book:

Martha Beals, Dorothy Blakey, Laure Mieskowski, Lisa Polzin and Lynda Zeller.

I am indebted to those who provided endorsements for this book: Dr. Phil Amerson, Bill Bode, Liz Bode, Dr. Kim Cape, Bishop Ken Carter, DeAnn Forbes Ervin, Rev. Susan Hagans, Judy Hahn, Dr. Ellsworth Kalas, Bishop Donald Ott and Margaret Valade.

Rev. Faith Fowler's ministry at Cass Community Social Services in Detroit and Cass Community United Methodist Church has been an inspiration to me. I am thrilled that this book is published by Cass Community Publishing House as an imprint of David Crumm Media, LLC.

The support and expertise of Read the Spirit founder David Crumm as well as his publishing colleagues at David Crumm Media, LLC enabled this book to come to a reality. They include Dmitri Barvinok, Celeste Dykas, Cody Harrell, John Hile and Rick Nease.

Most of all, I am grateful for tender mercy of God's love, the unfailing grace of Jesus the Christ, and the fierce sweetness of the Holy Spirit, which remind me to play and sustain me along the Way.

Praise for *Recess: Rediscovering Play and Purpose*

This book inspires me. The Rev. Laurie Haller leads by example through the many dangers, toils and snares of today's pastoral life and work. She is a marathon runner, physically and spiritually, and will help clergy reclaim their first love of Christ that fuels their own faithful passion for ministry. In "Recess" Haller captures what sustains us through our "quivering mass of availability" to what Eugene Peterson calls, "A Long Obedience in the Same Direction."

Dr. Kim Cape, General Secretary of the General Board of Higher Education and Ministry of The United Methodist Church.

* * *

Laurie Haller is one of the most disciplined and gifted leaders in our church. In Recess, she shares her own pilgrimage of how a very intentional and focused pastor navigates through seasons of challenge, chaos and complexity. I was profoundly moved by her self-awareness, and how this knowledge has shaped her life and ministry.

Ken Carter, Resident Bishop, Florida Area, The United Methodist Church

The idea of constant availability isn't unique to clergy—but extends to all humans who are hard-wired to create, serve, perform and offer care without end. Those of us who struggle with hard stops know the spiritual void that can follow when we simply give too much of ourselves away ...

From Fly Fishing to Taize in France—we walk (and run) with Laurie Haller as she navigates her spiritual journey.

Her ability to absolutely reveal herself, impediments and all, makes her your immediate friend. Her courage to stop, in the height of her career, without regard to social pressure, is nothing less than courageous. One finishes the book feeling hopeful and inspired—with only 'Recess' on the mind.

DeAnn Forbes, Vice President, Driven Communications

* * *

This unique look back at the work and ministry of Laurie Haller is also a great snapshot back for many of us as we lived through some of the same experiences. Laurie's glimpse back at her life through family and ministry is so well written she takes the rest of us with her, through her thoughts, concerns, trials and faith. "Recess" is a great read and study guide for any Adult Education class or small group. Take a moment, a 'recess' if you will, to join Laurie Haller and rediscover play and purpose.

Bill Bode, Christian Education Director, Grand Rapids, Michigan

* * *

I thoroughly enjoyed reading Laurie Haller's "Recess" manuscript. I was at once drawn into Laurie's stories by her easy writing style and interesting subject matter. I believe this book has broad appeal, especially to anyone who has ever taken time away to reflect on their life. Laurie's experiences, many of which she shared with her family, make a thought-provoking read, perfectly suited for a small group book study.

Liz Bode, Administrative Assistant, Grand Rapids District, West Michigan Conference, The United Methodist Church

"In the words of a Native American teacher, Harvey Swift Deer, every human being has both a survival dance, and a sacred dance." With these words, United Methodist clergywoman Laurie Haller begins her introspective journey from burnout and depression, through a place of holy waiting, into the recovery of her passion for ministry. This book will be encouragement for any person who is struggling to find God in the midst of the unrelenting demands of a servant life. From fly fishing in Montana, to finding God on the golf course, to praying with the Taize Community in France, Laurie journals her experiences in her sacred dance of becoming whole again. An easy read, this book will challenge all of us to look at our own struggles with new understanding.

Rev. Susan Hagans, Retired clergy, West Michigan Conference

* * *

In her book Recess, Laurie Haller offers a candid and compelling window into the complex and overwhelming world of parish leadership. If you are a pastor, a lay leader or one who cares about imaginative and faithful parish ministry, this is an essential resource for you. Laurie tells her story of duties and commitments that can wear one down, burn one out and cause one to give too much. This, danger faced by all of us who experience a call to be in service with others, is all too common. It leaves too many in brokenness, despair and a decision to abandon our "first love." In these pages is the honest account of spiritual and vocational renewal. Here is a thoughtful pastor telling of the move from weariness and despair to the joy of rest, play and establishing realistic commitments rooted in spiritual practices. In these pages one sees pastoral integrity in the making.

Dr. Philip Amerson, President Emeritus, Garrett-Evangelical Theological Seminary

Finding our own true path in this world is solitary work. Laurie has written so lucidly of her journey that it can help any of us along. I found inspiration, encouragement and motivation in her words. As she digs into her life, it is much more than a Sabbatical story; it is a beautiful, sometimes humorous, oftentimes painful insight into her life story.

This soul-searching journal of her sabbatical and how she strives to reconnect with her true self, God's child, is an inspiring and insightful story that might help any one of us on our individual journeys of self-discovery and awareness. She says, "Many of us expend so much time and energy in the survival dance that we never get to the sacred dance."

In expressing her gratitude, she writes "It was a gift I will only be able to repay by living the lessons that I learned about myself and about the church." This book is her gift to all of us. "Nothing that I do in this renewal leave can be called spiritual if it does not help other people become more faithful servants in the world." Mission accomplished, Laurie!

Margaret Valade, Member, Birmingham FUMC

* * *

I belong to a generation that didn't know there was such a thing as sabbaticals for the clergy. At that time, in fact, sabbaticals were still relatively rare in the academic world. Now, many years removed from my nearly forty years as a pastor, I applaud the idea.

But the sabbatical concept is only as good as the vision and character of the person exercising it. Laurie Haller takes us on the full journey, from the need that drove her to seek a grant, through the disciplines of the grant itself (a sabbatical is not an extended vacation), the living out-and-up of those months, and her summary evaluation more than a decade later. Her report is very readable and wonderfully candid. She dares to let us into her soul; indeed, she dares to let herself into her soul.

Any dedicated pastor might find her book valuable. Some, to determine if they need a sabbatical and don't know it, others who think they do but aren't really ready for it, and still others who are planning on one and who need to hear from a pilgrim who has already made the journey profitably. For the rest of us, her book is a valuable exercise in examining our own souls, and asking ourselves if there might be a way — long or short — for us to go deeper, wider, and higher in our journey of faith.

Dr. J. Ellsworth Kalas, Former President, Asbury Theological Seminary, Senior Professor of Homiletics.

* * *

Call it a book if you must, but for me *Recess* reads like a deeply revealing diary. Laurie Haller has a remarkable gift of linking everyday occurrences to her deep, yet always seeming elusive desire to always, everywhere, and with everyone, live with and like Jesus. As she says, "I have to keep reminding myself that the one thing necessary is to love God ..."

Laurie Haller's journal-based reflection on her three-month "leave" ("recess" as she calls it) from being full-time pastor/mother/spouse/daughter challenged me to examine my life and loves. Her revealing honesty and evident integrity are engagingly revealed in quotations from her valued mentors, her daily prayers and self-examination. "I try to fix with words things that cannot be fixed." (I am experiencing) ... "intensive loneliness, absolute emptiness, complete disconnection from anything familiar."

The Bighorn River in Montana, Hilton Head Island, Paris, the Taize community and a mid-recess return to her home community, sans responsibilities, provide the unfamiliar settings for self-examination. Laurie Haller's life is that of any person seeking to be all that God intends for us. Her "recess" is also the time she seeks to make a deliberately unsettling engagement with the legion of personal demons which pull us all away from God's intensions. In reading her "of the moment" reflections we meet some of our own demons, especially in the pastoral office. Among those she names are the dilemmas of parenting, the want for attention, the need to be needed, the seeking after importance, the fear of the unknown and obsession with work, with an inability to play ... even, I would add, at her "recess."

I urge you to read *Recess* by first jumping ahead to the late pages; those of "Chapter 13 -Reentry." They are a recital of the "vows" she pens at the end of this journey. In this way you will more readily note the multitude of gifts of recess grace that birthed her new vows ... among them ... the visit of Sarah and Talitha, the travel disruptions of 9/11, the chance meeting of Marcie and the threshold moment, especially the threshold moment, of the touch of forehead to cross.

Bishop Donald A. Ott

Preface

WE LIVE IN a world in which busyness and twenty-four hour availability are becoming the norm. Many articles and books have been written during the past decade applauding and critiquing this subject, yet rarely does an author seek to engage the reader in the personal struggle to identify the effects of too much activity and the hard work of coming to terms with it. Even rarer is the choice of the writer to be vulnerable with the reader in sharing a faith journey that becomes transformative.

In her book *Recess: Rediscovering Play and Purpose*, Laurie Haller has written with candor and honesty about her ongoing journey to wholeness. Aware that her life in ministry was leading to burnout, she had the courage to seek out time for a three-month leave in order to regain her passion for life. Taking time out sounds appealing and restful. Yet faced with the gift of time and lack of the previous activities in which she invested herself beyond limits, Laurie had to face what each person taking life seriously must encounter: oneself. This is no easy task, for solitude and silence have a way of confronting us with a truth that cannot be obtained in the hustle and bustle of our frenetic society.

In many ways our society has 'canonized' busyness. Work production is often measured in quantity rather than quality. Individuals who achieve are given more time-consuming responsibilities. Recent studies have shown that many workers often do not take full advantage of the amount of vacation time given and choose to stay in the workplace or at home in front of the computer screen. Is our sense of leisure becoming a lost art? Does the temptation to busyness diminish our desire for prayer, reflection, thinking or writing? How often do we hear individuals state that their days have been busy with lists to accomplish and tasks to perform! How rarely do we hear that one is busy contemplating underlying values that affect choices or that one is choosing solitude to sit with God and listen to the pulse of one's own life and one's connection with all life held in the embrace of the Divine. To choose a centered life is not always understood in our present day milieu, yet what would our world be like if more chose to live in an appreciation of our oneness rather than focus on differences that breed separation?

The complexities and busyness of daily life are as present to those who are in ordained ministry or any call to service. The perceptions may be that these individuals are exempt from the stressors listed above. After all, are not they doing God's work? To read the Gospel of Mark in one sitting may leave one with the impression that even Jesus lived a frenetic pace of life. Upon closer examination, however, we notice that he would take the time to go apart to commune with his Father. Our curiosity is spiked as we wonder what his experience in those holy encounters might be. It would seem that these times deepened his awareness of his identity and affirmed his sense of mission as he continued the journey to Jerusalem to embrace that which would occur in the days ahead.

In my ministry of spiritual direction, I have often listened to the stories of those involved in ministry. In these stories they relate feelings of a strong disconnect with their lives of discipleship, citing the lack of time and energy to integrate the message and mission of Jesus into their own lives. Recognizing the 'chronic emptiness' of her own spirit, Laurie made the choice to withdraw from the normal day to day routines and seek the God who invited her to look at her life, her spirit. Reading the table of contents in the book, one notices the profound movements from disengagement and floundering to the freedom to be able to waste time with Jesus, leading her to a transformation of spirit rooted in the Word of God. For Laurie the journey was a profound experience of self-knowledge and an understanding of her relationship with God.

While spending time with *Recess*, the reader will notice that the spiritual journey necessitates growth in self-knowledge as well as trust in a deepening relationship with God. The two are essential. What we see in Laurie's writing is her intentional growth in self-knowledge, especially as she faces what she calls her work obsession. Coupled with that is her growing openness to the transforming power of God silently happening as she says 'yes.' There is a noticeable movement in Laurie's writings during her sabbatical from awareness of inadequacies to the powerful experience of knowing she is loved for who she is, as she is. Ingrained messages of duty and performance are melted away. Self-acceptance before God is humbling, yet it is this stance that makes one more available to others and for ministry.

Laurie Haller chose to embrace life-giving questions during her three-month sabbatical. For her it was indeed a mountain-top experience. And, as with any such experience, the coming down from the mountain into the ordinary of each day is fertile ground for the deepening of relationship with God. Anyone who has been in relationship is most likely familiar with this movement. Laurie's desire to integrate her desert experience into daily life and ministry is well expressed in her final chapter. The Epilogue written years afterwards reminds us that the God of great consolation will also be the consoling Presence in times of suffering. No longer is the message "What can I do for God?" but "What will I allow God to accomplish in this world through me?"

Recess: Rediscovering Play and Purpose is an engaging reflection, not only for those in ministry, but for all intent on living a life where discernment or awareness of God's action in one's life and in the world becomes the basis for choices and responses. This book is for all of us who desire to have a listening heart that exudes the compassion and mercy of God. This is a book that inspires the reader to look at one's own life and ask similar questions that evoke honesty, integrity and a 'yes' to the grace offered by the Creator.

Judith Hahn
Grand Rapids, MI

Judy Hahn lives, works, prays and plays in Grand Rapids, Michigan. She is involved in the ministry of Spiritual Direction and also meets with individuals for counseling as a Clinical Social Worker.

Introduction

IT COULD HAVE gone either way. I could have easily dropped out, never to return to the professional ministry, another casualty in a profession that is not always kind to its clergy. Burned out, depressed and unsure of my call, I was no longer able to endure the incessant demands of pastoral ministry. I had forgotten who God created me to be and had become disconnected from my true self.

Knowing that all organizations need to reinvent themselves every five to seven years in order to remain vital, I realized that I was at a crossroads. At different times I found myself discouraged, bored, hopeless, depressed, beyond exhaustion, cynical, despairing, and numb. I was hanging on by a thread. Most of all, I had lost my joy and all semblance of balance between career, family and self.

Life is a continual process of change and growth. Yet in the lifecycle of my ministry, I had plateaued. Could I reinvent myself through adaptive and systemic personal transformation, or would I give up and find a job that did not dog me 24 hours a day?

Author, psychologist and psychotherapist Bill Plotkin writes in his book *Soulcraft* about Harvey Swift Deer, a Native American teacher who says that every human being has both a survival dance and a sacred dance. The survival dance, which occupies the first half of our life, is what we are paid to do to make a living. When we leave our parents' home, we need to find a way to become self-reliant and support ourselves physically and economically.

By contrast, the sacred dance is what we are called to do to live well—the work and/or play that nourishes our soul. Many of us expend so much of our time and energy in the survival dance that we never get to the sacred dance. The sacred dance is not about ego, money, status, power or advancement. It's about wholeness, passion, fullness of life and kingdom living.

The survival dance and the sacred dance are often not one and the same. Once we find a way to survive in this world, we are then free to develop our sacred dance. The danger for clergy is that the survival dance and the sacred dance become so intertwined that we cannot distinguish between the two. The focus of our calling becomes "building a career" that is so consuming that the holiness of the sacred dance becomes lost.

Twelve years ago I had the privilege of taking a three-month renewal leave from my responsibilities as a local church pastor in The United Methodist Church. Realizing that the stress and constant demands of 20 years of pastoral ministry had taken a toll on my physical, emotional and spiritual health, I applied for and received a $30,000 grant from the Lilly Endowment as part of their Clergy Renewal Program. It was a gift I will only be able to repay by living the lessons that I learned about myself and about the church.

Recess is the story of how I recovered play and purpose. It's a testimony to three months that saved my ministry, my sacred dance and my life.

—*Laurie Haller, 2014*

Snapping turtle: Laurie's first catch
ever with a fishing rod.

CHAPTER 1

Disengagement

THE DAY IS finally here! August 31, 2001. I can't believe it. I have a three-month renewal leave from my ministry as co-pastor of First United Methodist Church in Grand Rapids, Michigan. I don't know what to think or feel. I am not anxious or afraid anymore. I don't feel much of anything.

O God, I'm just tired.

My husband, Gary, with whom I co-pastor First Church, asked last night what I was thinking, and I simply said, "I'm tired." I also feel numb. How am I supposed to feel when leaving my children, husband and church for three months? Part of me says I'm making the biggest mistake of my life. Another part says, *OK, this is just the first day. Give yourself a chance.*

The first part of my renewal leave is a fly fishing trip with my father, Gerry Hartzel, on the Bighorn River in Montana. I meet him at the airport in Billings, Montana. On the drive to Fort Smith I can't help but notice how dry it is. They say at the trout shop that it hasn't rained for 40 days. I think about the dryness in my own life. For 20 years I gave and gave and gave to the people in my churches but did not allow myself to receive in return. I did work half time for eight years to be with my three young children, Sarah, Garth and Talitha, but ministry is never part time. It's a continual struggle to know what to do and what to let go.

When my youngest child, Talitha, was 3, I decided to pastor full time. I put my heart and soul into my appointed county seat church. It was the best match possible between pastor and congregation and the church thrived. But I wore myself out. I did little to take care of myself.

Four years later, Gary and I were asked to come to First Church, a downtown, urban congregation of 900 members. When I heard that First Church had come upon tough times and needed strong pastoral leadership, I could only think: *How in the world am I going to find the energy to do this? I am burned out now. I need a break now. How can I do this?*

We moved on the last Monday in June 1993, only a day after my farewell at the church I had served for four years. I was emotionally drained and physically exhausted. The moving van was coming, and I wasn't ready. Monday night we slept on the floor of our new house, on Tuesday our furniture arrived and was unloaded, and on Wednesday we made our first home visit to a parishioner recovering from surgery.

The next day we both started working full time, yet we didn't even have a chance to say adequate goodbyes to our former congregation! I would never do it that way again, but Gary and I both felt that our new church had invested a lot of hope in us. We believed we needed to give all we had to turn First Church around. It did happen, but at a cost. I gave too much.

Those who trust in the Lord are blessed. They are like trees planted by water, sending out their roots. They will not wilt when things get hot, and their leaves shall stay green; even in times of drought they will not become anxious but will continue to bear luscious fruit.

(Jeremiah 17:7-8)

* * *

Our fishing guide on the first day is John, who is teaching me how to fly fish. Most of all, he is teaching me the importance of waiting. Wait at the top of your cast before you throw it out. Snap, wait, throw, stop. He says that in fly fishing you don't follow through, which runs contrary to almost everything else in life, where follow-through is the key to success. You have to stop the rod at the 1:00 p.m position or else the fly will not go very far. And you can't snap your wrist. It's in the elbow. It takes me a while to get the hang of casting, but I learn enough to hook and land several trout.

I like how John says that each day on the river is different. The sun, clouds, wind, air and water temperature, currents, water flow and angle of the sun all affect the fishing. How true it is for humans as well.

Each day is different, a unique gift from God. Now if I can only live as if each day is a gift. Enjoy the moment!

Today certainly is a gift. The water temperature is 45 degrees, and the air temperature is 95 degrees. It's nice to stand in my waders in the frigid water yet feel the warmth of the hot sun. As I relax in the boat at the end of the day, I begin to reflect on the weeks leading up to my renewal leave.

I was pretty strung out those last days, trying to get everything done before I left. I had my two older children to get ready for college, my youngest to prepare for her sophomore year in high school and countless details to take care of in order to hand off my church responsibilities to others for the fall.

I wrote in my journal on August 26:

I've been feeling pretty stressed about my renewal leave. My list seems to grow longer and longer, and I wonder if I'm going to get it all done. A friend prayed that I might know what to let go and not worry about. I hope I can do it.

I notice that I've been losing weight the last several weeks. I think my metabolism has shifted into high gear, and I am moving so fast from one thing to another that I'm not thinking straight, either. I'm forgetting things. I'm continually making wrong turns when driving. And I could not remember the kind of candy one of my friends likes so much. I stood in the grocery store looking at every single brand of candy and simply could not identify the one she likes. I thought of Alzheimer's disease. My mother's brother died of Alzheimer's in his 70s, and I am very aware that it runs in families. I trust that after I take off on my leave, my mind will clear.

A week before I left, I played golf for the last time with Gary and our neighbor John. My tee-shot on the first hole was pathetic. I hit another one, which was worse. In frustration, I threw my 3 wood as high in the air as I could, and it almost hit John on the way down. Amazingly, it didn't break. After that shameless display, I realized that I was under stress and probably would not be playing well, so I settled down.

To be fair, my anxiety did not only revolve around making preparations to leave, but I wondered about the wisdom of leaving at all. I first thought about a renewal leave in December 1999 when I experienced a mild depression. I plodded mechanically through my responsibilities but experienced little joy.

I decided that my depression was a combination of factors. Our oldest daughter, Sarah, had experienced an awful four years of high school. She was in and out of trouble and in and out of hospitals. I cannot begin to describe the pain and horror of that time for our entire family. That Christmas, Sarah took her final English class so she could receive her high school diploma and I think I just fell apart. The stress of having to take care of her and keep everything else together at home and church was an incredible strain. I was just beginning to allow myself to feel that pain.

A second contributing factor was that we had just completed our second major remodeling project at the church. Gary and I were deeply involved in these projects. We worked on the plans with highly capable lay people but did much of the personal fundraising ourselves. It took a toll, but even more disconcerting was the thought: *Now that we've spent all this money remodeling the church, what are we going to do with it? What is our mission now that the church looks good, and many outside groups want to use it?*

I sensed we were in a holding pattern, waiting for God to give us new vision as a congregation. I am not good at waiting, however, so the question was nagging at me as we approached the year 2000. Where were Gary and I going to lead First Church? Gary is more relaxed about such questions, but even if God is giving direction, our congregation looks to us.

The third factor was simple burnout. I had worked nonstop for 18 years in ministry, and I was tired, bone-weary and dried up. I knew I couldn't continue at that pace much longer. I had no more to give. I needed a break, a long break.

My depression continued into mid-January, when Gary and I went to Florida for an education conference. As I ran along the beach one morning, I was startled by a bright orange-yellow shell lying along the water. No other shells of that color appeared anywhere else on the beach. I picked it up, and suddenly God said to me, "Brighten up!" (This is a variation on the words I often hear from others, "Lighten up, Laurie!") To this day, I carry that shell in my purse.

Around this time, I broached the subject of a renewal leave with Gary, explaining that the only way I was going to survive as a pastor was to take an extended break from the ever-present demands of ministry. Gary was receptive, so we began talking with our church's Pastor-Parish Relations Committee, whose dual role is to evaluate and support the pastors. They were very encouraging of the idea, so I began to do some serious thinking about timing and what I might actually do. It was pretty scary to think about leaving my children, home and church. It also seemed incredibly selfish. However, God planted a seed that began to take root and grow.

All of this sounded great a year ago, or even six months ago. Now that the time is actually here, though, I am afraid—not just of leaving my family and church, but afraid of what I might discover about myself.

* * *

While jogging this morning in Montana, God gave me this word: "recess." What I am doing now is taking a recess from the normal routines of living.

When I was a little girl, recess was my favorite subject. I loved being outside and playing every game imaginable. I never liked being indoors and playing with dolls. I never even owned a doll.

In elementary school, my weekly piano lessons with Mr. Bartholomew were during lunch recess. I ate lunch at the school, and then walked to Mr. Bartholomew's house. The problem was, I loved recess so much that I couldn't keep my mind on the piano and continually looked out the window toward the playground. I didn't last too long with Mr. Bartholomew.

What happened to that joyful and carefree little girl? Now I find it so difficult to play. Having fun can be excruciatingly painful. All I seem to do is work. And when I do have an hour to play, I work at my play. I have an inner drive to be productive, even now during this renewal leave. Part of me believes

I must have something to show after three months, or it won't be worth all the sacrifices other people had to make in order for me to be gone.

We have another good day on the river. Our guide is Steve, who will be with us for the next four days. One comment John said yesterday has helped me today. When we began dry fly fishing on the surface of the water, he insisted that I had to follow the fly. He said the only way I could know I had hooked a fish was to see the fly disappear. I was used to fishing by feel. When you feel a tug, pull up on the line.

At first, I could not see the fly float down the river. After all, the fly looked just like all the other flies that were hatching and floating down the river. I despaired of ever being able to follow the fly. But, by the end of the day, I was beginning to track my fly and was more successful at fishing.

How important it is to be able to truly see. That's a weak area of my ministry. I have to work to focus solely on those whom I counsel or visit in the hospital or nursing home. I have to see them as children of God and let go of everything else that is distracting me and floating around in my head. By giving them my entire attention, I have to treat them as if no one else exists at that moment.

* * *

A resource I am using in my devotional time while on leave is *A Guide to Retreat for All God's Shepherds*, by Reuben Job. A friend gave it to me for this purpose. The preface is so apropos it is scary. Job writes that we are so enslaved to the demands of each day that are not even aware of how empty we are in our spirit. I think my depression in December 1999 was a recognition of the chronic emptiness within my spirit. If I hadn't gone through that experience, I probably would not be on this renewal leave today.

In Chapter 1, Job talks about "ineffable moments" and "the dark night of the soul" as contrasting states of the spirit. Ineffable moments are mountaintop experiences, those times in life when we are totally at one with ourselves and with God. We are complete, whole children of God. I have had many such ineffable experiences in my life:

- Singing J.S. Bach's *Mass in B minor* in the Basilica of Vezelay in France in 1975 with a choir from West Berlin, Germany.
- My wedding in 1978.
- An organ recital I gave at my home church, Zion Mennonite Church, in Souderton, Pennsylvania in 1979.
- My first 10-kilometer race on May 4, 1980.
- The birth of our three children: Sarah in 1981, Garth in 1983 and Talitha in 1986.
- My ordination in 1982.
- My first marathon in 1984.
- A First Church mission trip to Cuba in 1997.
- Running in my first Boston marathon in 1999.

On the other hand, the dark nights of the soul are those occasions—often at night—when I feel utter despair and hopelessness. Fortunately, those times have not come along too often—but they have been excruciating when they have occurred:

- My night of agony in 1975 when I finally said yes to God and had a conversion experience.
- The period of four and a half months during my first pregnancy when I was so sick I considered both abortion and suicide.
- The Saturday night when one of our active teenagers drowned in the local lake, and I had to preach the next morning after spending much of the night with the boy's mother.
- The night one of our children ran away.

- The time, several years ago, when I was out of state at a conference and received a crisis call from home and another one from a church member. I spent the night in pure agony, despairing about my family, my beloved church members and my vocation.

I used to fight the emptiness, but now I understand the mountains and the valleys to be complementary. Without valleys, there can be no mountains. Without great pain, there cannot be great joy. Without great evil, there cannot be great good. Now I am learning to go with the emptiness, to embrace it, to allow it to penetrate my very being. Only then can I move on.

It's like catching a rainbow trout. Rainbows are known for being fighters. They are not easy to land. Because we can only catch and release on the Bighorn River, the rainbows are going to be set free. So the best thing for a rainbow that is hooked is not to fight the fisherman but allow itself to be landed. That way it will be released sooner. If the rainbow fights, it will just take longer to land, making the whole experience more painful.

* * *

Dad asks if I am relaxed by now, and I honestly say yes. I'm feeling great and am tremendously enjoying being outside all day and learning a new skill. For the first time I feel as if I've "got it" as far as fly fishing goes.

The easy part of fly fishing is called "nymphing," which is sort of like trolling. The boat drifts, and we cast off the side of the boat with a split shot and an indicator on the line. When the yellow or orange indicator goes under the surface, it means a fish has been hooked and the rod needs to be jerked upward. This does not involve much skill as far as placement of the cast is concerned.

On the other hand, dry fishing happens when the fly stays on top of the water and the fish rise to eat the fly. The challenge is twofold. First, you have to aim the cast about five feet upstream of a fish rising to the surface. You have to target an individual fish or you won't catch anything. Second, you have to watch the fly move downstream. If the fly disappears, it means a fish has taken it. You cannot rely on feel for this. You have to watch. Of course, with thousands of PMDs (pale morning duns or mayflies) floating on the surface, it's almost impossible to spot the fly.

This afternoon I finally catch two fish on my own by casting right toward a rising fish, watching the fly disappear and then jerking on the line. That is what purists call real fly fishing—wading in the river and dry fishing.

Of course, there are wonderful parallels between dry fishing and fishing for people to bring into the church. We are told over and over to have a target audience. You can't just send out mass mailings to any old place. You can't start a new worship service without knowing whom you want to reach. Specialization is the name of the game the world over today.

I really do admire specialists. Our guide, Steve, is a specialist. He is an expert on the 13-mile stretch of the Bighorn River north of Fort Smith, Montana. He knows every inch of that river. He knows all the nooks and crannies. He knows the various insects that the trout eat. He knows how the river changes in different seasons. It's phenomenal, and I respect his thorough knowledge of the Bighorn River.

In contrast, as a pastor, I see myself as a generalist. I know a little bit about a lot of different things, but I'm not an expert in anything. That's frustrating for a self-proclaimed perfectionist. I get angry at myself because I don't have the time to learn skills in depth and do anything extremely well.

I am convinced, however, that local church pastors have to be generalists. We must be good at pastoral care. We have to feel comfortable in nursing homes and hospitals. We have to know how to listen well. We are expected to be able to preach a sermon that is interesting, conveys truth about God and inspires people to action and transformation. We must be able to teach children, youth and adults. We have to counsel people whose marriages are dissolving, who are getting married, who face career changes, who are depressed, who are questioning their faith and who are unemployed.

We have to be extroverted and "press the flesh" at coffee hour after church. We have to be able to make cold phone calls and visits to prospective members. We have to be able to manage a staff. We have to be good at organization. We have to be able to identify and train laypersons for leadership. We have to be a presence in the community. We have to officiate at funerals, weddings and baptisms and say prayers at civic functions. We have to be able to lead a meeting. We have to be fundraisers. We have to go to people's homes and ask for money for special projects or capital campaigns. We have to write well. Above all, we have to love our people. That's a lot, and it makes me weary just thinking about it.

Thank you, Jesus that I don't have to do any of those tasks for three months. Yes, I believe I am beginning to disengage.

* * *

I keep getting up early—real early. I have always been an early riser, but the two-hour time change also makes a difference. I have time for devotional reading before I go out for my morning run. This morning I read Luke 4:18-19, where, at the beginning of his ministry, Jesus travels back to his hometown, Nazareth. He then goes to the synagogue and unrolls the scroll of the prophet Isaiah. He reads: "The Spirit of the Lord rests upon me, because he has called me to bring good news to the poor. He has sent me to proclaim release to the prisoners and recovery of sight to the blind, to let the oppressed go free, to proclaim God's kingdom."

This is Jesus' mission statement! His purpose and goal is to preach good news to the poor. Unfortunately, his own people are filled with rage and drive him out of town.

Then I read Romans 12:1: "So here's what I hope you will do, with God's mercy undergirding you. Take your one, ordinary life and present it to God as offering."

Reading this passage reminds me that I wrote a personal mission statement four years ago. It was during a time when I was mightily struggling with priorities and needed a different way to think about my ministry. I keep it in my Day-Timer. It reads: **"My mission is to serve God and make a positive difference in the world by taking care of myself and my family, ministering in my local church and working to bring in the kingdom for all of God's children."**

My primary mission is to serve God. I am totally committed to making a positive difference in the world by everything I do. I am convinced that nothing I am or do can be called spiritual or "Christian" if it does not help other people to become more faithful servants in the world. The difficult question is: How do I accomplish that mission? I know that I need to take care of myself. I need to exercise, which I do faithfully. I need to get enough sleep, which is a problem. I need to care for my spirit, which is another challenge.

Next is my family. The needs of my family must come before the needs of my church. It is only in the last five years that my eyes have been opened to this truth. Nurturing three teenagers and being there for them is more important now than when they were little. I remember whining and moaning about how difficult it was to care for small children when I only worked part time and was the primary caregiver. I felt trapped in the house a lot and could never seem to get any time for myself. Everyone told me that it's nothing compared to having teenagers, but I couldn't see it—until now. Caring for young children is physically draining, but caring for teenagers is emotionally and spiritually draining.

I also work hard at making time to spend with Gary apart from work. Because we are colleagues, we see each other a lot. We are in constant communication professionally, but that is no substitute for taking time to nurture our marriage. We carefully plan to take a day off together and rework our schedules to use all of our vacation time. My family is more important than my job.

After family comes the local church. I have struggled in the past eight years with how to be a presence in the Grand Rapids community. Our church wants its pastors to be actively involved in community affairs, but I've discovered that is not part of my individual mission statement. It's not that I don't want to be involved. I simply need to take care of my family, my church and myself first.

Whenever I am asked to take on another responsibility, I pull out my mission statement and ask: *Where does this fit in with my mission?* If it doesn't fit, I will usually say no. If I say yes, I will become more overcommitted than I already am, and nothing will be done well. My only desire is to take my one, ordinary life and place it before God as an offering. At the end of my renewal leave, I intend to review my mission statement and make any necessary changes.

* * *

What a day! I hook 21 fish and land 13, far better than any other day. What a great way to disengage from pastoral ministry!

Once on the river, we decide to go down a 13-mile stretch for the first time. Some guides don't want to go that far because there is mostly nymph fishing (few PMDs are on the surface). The river is also littered with moss, so we have to constantly clean our lines. In the morning, we have moderate success nymphing on the upper three miles. Then, after lunch we dry fish in our waders for a while. I am getting more comfortable every day with dry fishing. Today, I catch only one fish that way, but I am proud that I aimed correctly and the fish took the fly. Dad, the ultimate fisherman, is not having much luck either.

The real surprise is that when we reach the lower 10 miles, we start catching fish like crazy. I am astounded! I keep getting bites, hooking fish and landing them. I even catch two whitefish, which are considered junk fish on the Bighorn.

All in all, it is a very good day. I am really having a wonderful time. It's difficult to believe I actually have three months of this. I find myself not thinking so much. I am simply "being." I relish being outside watching everything going on around me. I also enjoy talking with Steve and other natives to this area. What a different life this is, yet these are people just like those in Grand Rapids, with hopes, dreams, heartaches and a longing for God.

* * *

In the middle of the night, I wake up from a bad dream in which I am being attacked in my hotel room. I'd had a nagging fear before going to bed that it would be easy for someone to come in my room at night because there is no dead bolt. I try not to let those fears run away with me, but evidently my subconscious could not let it go.

Like most people, I battle certain fears on a regular basis. My two biggest fears are dogs and elevators. Years ago, I was attacked by a pit bull as I was running. The dog rushed out from behind a house on a country road and I didn't have a prayer of escaping. Fortunately, a teenage boy from a neighboring house was outside and saw what was happening. He took a baseball bat and beat the dog away from me. Ever since, I have had an irrational fear of dogs, especially when running in rural areas.

I also have a fear of enclosed spaces. When I was a little girl, I became stuck in a bathroom on the beach at Ocean City, New Jersey, where our family vacationed every summer. I simply could not get the door unlocked and ended up climbing over the top of the door. Since then, the fear of enclosed places has become a well-developed claustrophobia in my life.

I am terrified of most elevators because there are no windows, they are small, and I can't even begin to imagine being stuck between floors. When I get onto an elevator, I can feel my pulse begin to race, and I almost hyperventilate. Even now, as I am writing, I can feel the panic. I can't remember how many times I have gotten on an elevator only to hop off before the doors shut because of one thing or another: a strange noise, a jerking motion, no one else on the elevator, or just bad vibes. Because I don't have time to use the stairs every time I go to a hospital to visit a parishioner, I am gradually learning to face this fear, but it's not easy. As for the elevator at First Church, I haven't a clue what it even looks like inside. I won't go near it!

* * *

I've just returned from one of the most scenic runs I have ever taken. I overcame my fear of passing several houses with potential dogs and ended up running to the top of the Yellowtail Dam. I think my quadricep muscles will be sore tomorrow. About two miles are straight uphill. It is such a gorgeous morning. I saw the sunrise with brilliant orange light reflecting off the clouds. I ran along the canyon and observed all the vegetation, birds and shades of light.

I continue to relish this beautiful and barren land during our last day of fishing. The fishing is pretty good, considering the wind came up in the afternoon and stifled the dry fishing. I land some big rainbows today. It's great fun. We also experience clouds and some rain, even a rainbow in the late afternoon. Steve is a great guide, very professional and helpful, with a pleasant personality. What a perfect way to start my renewal leave.

I read an excerpt tonight from Robert J. Wicks' book, *Touching the Holy*, where he quotes a seminarian who heard Desmond Tutu speak. The student remarked, "Today I met a holy man." When asked to elaborate, the seminarian said that in Tutu's presence he was able to experience Christ in his own life. *If only I can be a window to Christ for others through my presence.*

I think of our guide, Steve, who says over and over, "Well done, Laurie. Well done, Gerry." That really makes me feel good even though I know I goof up more than I do well in fly fishing. I want to be that kind of affirming presence to others. I want people to feel peace, calm, serenity and comfort by being with me. But if I do not feel peace, calm, serenity and comfort in my interior life, I have nothing to offer to others, no matter how much I want to give.

Perhaps that is my goal for these three months: to listen to God, discover who I am underneath all the crud and then become the person God wants me to be.

Release

Suffocating in my own busyness I am
Drowning in my own self-importance.
I can no longer pull myself back onto dry ground.
Cast me not away from your presence, Lord,
Reel me into your kingdom.
Rest, hope, release from my own expectations;
Bathed in the light of your love;
I yearn for a new way of living and being.
My help is in the name of the Lord.
Dare I let go?

Ready to fly fish on the Bighorn River, Montana.

CHAPTER 2

Floundering

LAST NIGHT, AS I prayed, I thanked God that I have been able to disengage from pastoral ministry. I prayed for the congregation as I vowed to do daily during my renewal leave. However, during the night, I had a disturbingly familiar dream. Gary and I were at a worship service in another church. I don't believe I was preaching—I think Gary was—but there were many people there, and it was difficult making my way to the robing area where the choir was waiting. Others were also robing. Our seminary intern and director of senior high youth and young adults were among them. Someone asked what color stole we should wear, and I replied white. For some reason, I brought every robe and stole I owned to this event.

I pulled out the white robe that I used most often and was horrified to see that it had shrunk to half its size! Someone must have put it in the washing machine, because not only did it shrink, it was all wrinkled. I panicked for a moment, and then realized I had my other white robe. As I was putting it on, someone said a prayer with the choir. They began to process into the sanctuary. Meanwhile, I could not find my communion stole. All of my stoles were on the floor of the closet, but I simply could not find it, nor could I locate any white stole at all. As I frantically looked around, everyone else went into the sanctuary during the first hymn. After that, Gary walked back out of the sanctuary looking for me. I was still fumbling with all of my stoles when I woke up.

This dream is a variation on a common theme: not being prepared for worship. Often the dream will revolve around me not being prepared to preach. Either I have lost my manuscript or I am simply not ready to preach without my manuscript. I get up in front of everyone and am not able to talk. Nothing comes out of my mouth. I guess I really haven't let it all go yet.

The good news is that I wake up to rain, which this area of Montana has not seen for six weeks. The owner of the restaurant said last night that this is the worst drought since the dust bowl of the 30s.

Today, Dad and I fly to Denver, then on to Phoenix where we meet my mother, Gwen Hartzel, who arrives at the same time. We're going to spend six days together golfing and sightseeing.

I call home tonight, and Gary is at a meeting. I enjoy talking with our younger daughter, Talitha, and hearing about her cross-country team and high school. I feel a twinge of guilt, however, knowing that Gary is working so hard in my absence while I am out playing golf in Arizona. That leads to another round of questioning as to why I am taking this renewal leave at all.

In the summer of 2000, I applied for a grant from the Lilly Endowment, Inc., which had initiated a new program of awarding grants to local church pastors for renewal leaves. In December 2000, I was awarded the grant. This provided funding for me as well as for the church to hire pastoral assistance while I was gone. In the church's grant application, the Pastor Parish Relations Committee wrote that there would be four parts to my leave: disengagement from pastoral responsibilities, spiritual growth, reflection and service.

The first two weeks of the renewal leave in Montana and Arizona were meant simply to enjoy being with my parents, who live in another state and whom I do not see very often. Then I was to go to Taizé, France, a monastic community that welcomes pilgrims from all over the world for weekly stays. After that I was going to spend five weeks at Hilton Head, South Carolina, where I would rest, read and write. Finally, I would travel to Rwanda, Africa, for two weeks with a mission team from our church to help build a Methodist high school. I felt very strongly that, having spent so much time focused on myself, I wanted to reach out in service as well. I would spend the last two weeks at home wrapping up my writing and preparing for the onslaught of Advent and Christmas.

In my last sermon at First Church five days before I left, I created a theme from this André Gide quote: "One does not discover new lands without consenting to lose sight of the shore for a very long time." I concluded by saying this:

> *I am leaving on Friday for three months. I am going to lose sight of the shore for what seems right now to be a very long time. I do not intend to work or produce or stay the same. I intend to enlarge my borders. As I open myself to God's leading, I will seek to know God more deeply. I plan to assess my life, where I've been and where God wants me to go. Who knows? I may even invite some chaos into my life!*

My goal is to come back a more balanced and faithful person so that I can be a better witness of the love of Christ to all of God's children in this world. I want to thank each one of you for graciously providing me this time away, and I especially want to thank Gary for encouraging me and cheerfully taking on the extra work it will mean for him, not only at the church but at home as well. I also covet your prayers, as I have covenanted to pray daily for you. Remember: "One does not discover new lands without consenting to lose sight of the shore for a very long time."

* * *

Today, I decide it's time for an honest assessment of my life, beginning with my faults and failures. I believe that we must continually examine our lives. As Socrates reminded us centuries ago, "The unexamined life is not worth living." John Wesley, the founder of Methodism, believed that self-examination was critical for him as well as his leaders.

In their book, *Leading the Congregation*, Norman Shawchuck and Roger Heuser write how John Wesley set aside time every day for what he called "examination." Later in life he'd set Saturday apart for self-examination, and when he was elderly, Wesley would stop what he was doing for the first five minutes of each hour to examine the hour just passed. If we are not aware of our motives and our interior life, there is potential for trouble. This is especially true for pastors because the danger of fulfilling our own needs through our parishioners is great. I start examining myself on the airplane this morning by listing my shortcomings.

- I am an introvert. I receive energy from being alone, not from being with other people. At times I will withdraw from others when I need to be reaching out to them. I am thus perceived as unfriendly, standoffish and difficult to get to know. When I am "off duty" and out in the community, I have occasionally avoided people I know because I don't want to talk with them. I also distance myself from other parents at school because I don't have the energy to be talkative and outgoing after having to do this all day at church. Sometimes it takes a tremendous effort of the will to be gregarious. I have learned how to do it for my role as pastor, but it still does not come naturally to me, even after 20 years in the ministry.

- I speak hastily and glibly. I verbally try to fix problems that cannot be fixed. I attempt to provide answers when it is better to quietly hold a parishioner's hand. A sweatshirt I found at a Cracker Barrel restaurant says it better than I could: "Lord, keep your hand on my shoulder and your hand over my mouth."

- I expect too much of myself. I expect that I can work 14 hours a day, be a good wife and mother and take care of myself. I am filled with pride.

- I am too focused on doing. I cannot relax and rest. I have to physically leave town to be on vacation. If a church member is in the hospital, I feel I must go if I'm home even if someone else from the church is doing hospital visitations for us.

- I try to do too many things at once. I become distracted and do not give others my full attention.

- I hover over people too much and insist on checking up to make sure things are done. Sometimes it's just easier to do it myself.

- I am too disciplined and not spontaneous enough. I cannot leave things and go off and play if there is something yet to be done. I don't have enough fun.

- I don't smile enough.

- I am too intense and serious.
- I am too much of a realist, which can hinder dreaming.
- I have not cultivated an adequate support system around me.
- I want to make others into who I want them to be.
- I am too controlling.

I keep striving toward perfection, but if truth be told, some of these faults are ones that I don't want to work on or change right now. I am content with them. They are a part of me. How can I honestly confront those areas of my personality and life that need transformation? During this time away, I trust that through becoming more self-aware, cultivating spiritual disciplines and taking time for reflection, I can refine myself and become more Christ-like.

* * *

Gary calls at 6 a.m., 9 a.m. his time. He needs to talk about how difficult his week is and how busy and harried he is. At the same time, he apologizes for telling me those things and encourages me to have a good time with my folks. It is a sweet phone call, but on my run immediately afterward I have to work very hard to pray for the needs Gary mentioned and then let them go.

This afternoon I read a selection from Eugene Peterson's *Working the Angles*. He says that the three main jobs of a pastor are prayer, Scripture-reading and spiritual direction. Unfortunately, these things are not visible to a congregation. Therefore, the temptation is for the pastor to abandon them in favor of meetings, appointments, etc. After all, visible acts pay the bills and make parishioners happy.

In short, we sell our souls. That is exactly where I am. I confess that because no one begs me to attend to these three tasks, I neglect and even abandon them. I can get by for a long time without them. Tending to my spiritual life may mean I can't see Mr. Smith's mother in the hospital. It may mean that I can't teach a weekly class. It may mean that I can't attend a committee meeting. Until now, I have not been willing to make those difficult decisions. I want to be there for my parishioners all of the time.

Eventually, however, the lack of performing these three tasks catches up with pastors. If we're lucky, one day we will stop long enough to realize that we are completely empty. That's me. I hope this renewal leave will afford me the time to become reacquainted with God and myself. My role is to connect and coordinate what people do in their work and play with God's acts of mercy and justice in the world. That ought to be my calling, and I need to keep that continually in the forefront. However, I cannot do it if I am not attuned to my own spiritual life.

This afternoon Mom and I have a conversation about pastors and churches. My mother has been a faithful church member for more years than I can imagine, and she has always been loyal to her pastors. We talk about churches in their area of Pennsylvania and how her friends are always complaining about their pastors.

I look at these conversations a lot differently than do people who aren't pastors. I know how difficult it is to please everyone. I know how it feels to be criticized. I know what it's like to be raked up and down the coals. I remember such an experience in my first church. After I had been in a small, rural congregation for a few years, a special meeting of the Pastor Parish Relations Committee was called for a Sunday afternoon. The committee proceeded to present a laundry list of things I was doing wrong:

- Too much power: directs people too much.
- Too liberal: sermons not close enough to Scripture, should be less worldly.
- Lack of spontaneity in prayers.
- Not diplomatic.
- Not as compassionate as should be.

- Unfriendly; ignores people; cold; negative; aggressive.
- Not humble.
- Immature.
- Too young for the job.
- Child-care costs and responsibilities shouldn't be passed on to the congregation.
- Too free with money.
- Pushing too hard for parsonage.

Naturally, these criticisms stung, but some of them were true. I particularly remember preaching a hard-hitting sermon on peace and justice a month after I arrived—not a smart thing to do. One parishioner even called my district superintendent to complain.

The harshest criticism to hear was about child care. It was raised because a few months earlier I asked if church folks would be willing to provide child care for my two young children so I could lead a newly formed youth group. Of course, no one mentioned that in my half-time position, I volunteered to add this responsibility to my job description and put in extra time with the youth. At the same time, I was upfront about the fact that Gary also worked Sunday evenings as a youth leader in another church, and I simply had no child care. Since we wanted all of the teenagers to be in the youth group, we worked out a schedule so that parents would take turns watching my children.

What I heard from a young mother on the committee was, "All the rest of us who work have to pay for child care, so why shouldn't you?" It was not a good day, and I have kept that laundry list of complaints to keep me humble. Fortunately, we were able to talk honestly about the issues and work together to resolve them.

While serving another church, I gave birth to my third child. I was pregnant when we moved there and was working half time as an associate pastor. The women of the church were very kind and purchased a portable playpen that I could set up in my office during those first months after Talitha was born. It was especially useful for evening meetings. I could nurse Talitha, put her to bed, and then go back to my meeting.

How it hurt, then, when I heard through the grapevine that I was being criticized for bringing my baby to work and not being professional. Needless to say, I didn't bring Talitha to work very much after that. It only takes one or two people to take away all the joy of ministry.

Another time I became caught in the middle of two young mothers whose children were not getting along in church. They would each complain to me about the other woman's child, until one night I'd had enough. Both of them were in the building, so I brought them into my office where we all sat down together to work it out.

I thought it went well, but the next day I heard from the church's lay leader that one of the women involved accused me of physically forcing her to come into my office—she was talking about bringing charges against me. A few days later the lay leader and I went to her home, we talked, and the situation seemed to be resolved. A few weeks after that, I received one of those anonymous letters that clergy love so dearly. The writer claimed I was a horrible pastor and poor role model for the congregation because I could not control my three children on Sunday morning.

Yes, pastors are not perfect, but we can also be convenient scapegoats. Church members can blame the pastor for all sorts of things when their own lives are not going well. It's easy to understand intellectually but difficult to accept emotionally.

* * *

On my run this morning, I begin thinking about the fact that this renewal leave may be my mid-life crisis. I am halfway through my ministry, and Sarah, Garth and Talitha are in college and high school. It is a good time to assess where I am in life. Do I want the rest of my life to be like the first half? Do I want to continue in the same profession? Are there things

I regret not having done? Are there dreams I've had since childhood that I could still possibly accomplish? Is my life worthwhile? Am I making the most of the time I have? Am I using the gifts God has given me to their fullest?

I am aware that people cope with mid-life in different ways. Some changes are healthy; others are not. Some people decide to change careers and pursue a more satisfying vocation. Others step off the fast track and slow down, perhaps finding a less stressful job. Some folks take up a hobby and do something they never took the time to do earlier. Others attempt to satisfy a yearning for youth, like buying a sports car or a boat. Some people decide to end their marriage because they don't want to go through the rest of their life unhappy. Others have an affair with someone half their age or try to make themselves look 20 years younger.

This renewal leave is giving me the time to discover who I am before I take any action about where I should be heading and what I should be doing.

Lord, I really want to be open to your leading.

A Scripture that has new meaning for me today is Mark 6:30, where Jesus sends his disciples off in pairs to heal and exorcize demons. After they come back to Jesus and report, Jesus says, "Go off by yourselves. Take a break and get some rest." Jesus and his disciples don't even have time to eat. They get into a boat and head to a remote place, but the people arrive there before Jesus does! They are hungering so much for Jesus' teaching that he takes pity on them and goes right back to work and begins teaching them.

Do you see? Jesus had the same struggles between doing and being that we do. We must have time to ourselves for prayer, Bible study and personal reflection.

We also need to be people of action. How to balance them is the challenge. Reuben Job says that we struggle because our compassion prompts us to help others while our desire to be close to God beckons us to flee into the desert alone.

The tension will never go away. However, through the tension we can find a creative way to seek God's presence. Every day should have action, prayer and reflection. For me, however, the prayer and reflection have usually come after the action. While keeping a journal this past year, I saw how easy it was for me to leave it until the end of the day when I had no time or energy left.

I need to pay attention to my inward journey as well as my outward journey. During this renewal leave, my focus is inward. I know that I am not as effective when I lose my soul and allow it to sleep while my mind and heart race ahead. I am out of balance. I can't be a good leader and have the right vision for my church if I have lost my spirit.

* * *

Today my parents and I take a tour of Taliesin West, Frank Lloyd Wright's winter home. I learn that Wright began building Taliesin in 1937 when there was little else in the area. Today, Arizona loses 1.5 acres every hour of every day to new buildings. Metropolitan Phoenix is the fastest growing area in the country.

Wright called his work organic and was honest with his materials. He determined that none of his buildings would be higher than a desert tree so they would not overshadow nature.

We are taken into Wright's living room, which is one of the three most photographed rooms in the United States. According to our guide, Wright's wife said he absorbed everything he saw. That was the secret of his genius. Wright himself said that human beings should not go through life with closed fists. Rather, we should go through life with open palms in order to absorb everything.

Wright was not afraid to try and fail. Wright's "organic commandment," written in 1940, says: "Love is the virtue of the heart (circle). Sincerity is the virtue of the mind (square).

Courage is the virtue of the spirit (triangle). Decision is the virtue of the will (three lines)."

Our guide concludes the tour by saying that people sometimes ask, "What was Wright's religion?" She replies, "Wright believed that God could best be seen in nature."

Certainly, there is truth in that statement. So far in my renewal leave, I have reconnected with the out-of-doors, and I have seen God in so many ways by taking the time to observe and simply be at one with creation. However, I see God most clearly in other people, especially in those who show passion in their lives. I am reminded of a quote from Helen Keller, "Even more amazing than the wonders of nature are the powers of the spirit." Our guide is a good example. She is a beautiful woman, poised and confident, almost an actress in the way she talks about Wright. It is obvious that she reveres him, and her passion and spirit come through clearly.

I also observe passion in John and Steve, our fishing guides. It is people of passion who make the greatest difference in this world. They are so invested in what they are doing that God's handiwork is written all over their lives. The funny thing is, most of the time they are not even conscious of it.

As I observe myself and other colleagues in ministry, I would say that one thing we pastors often lack is passion. There is a boredom that comes from spiritual emptiness, which we disguise by being so busy that we avoid facing it. It's apathy of the soul, a burnout of the spirit that results in simply going through the motions of ministry without any passion or connection with God.

I pray for passion.

* * *

I go to church this morning with great expectations. I find a community church with an 8 a.m. service, which means I am in worship at the same time as most of my church members back home. I also know it's going to be difficult since today is Homecoming, one of the high Sundays in the life of First

Church. It's the first Sunday of church school, youth groups and high commitment study groups. It's also the first Sunday back in the sanctuary after it was painted and remodeled all summer. Finally, there is the consecration of a four-story office building that the church recently purchased across the street, along with a progressive dinner in the building, which Gary told me tonight has been named "First Place."

I am desperately hoping to feel connected to First Church by worshipping at the same time, but it doesn't work. I enter a gymnasium with chairs set up on the floor. A praise band plays the prelude, and the congregation claps afterward as if it were a performance. As I look over the bulletin, I notice that the 10 people listed as "The Leadership Team" are all men—six male pastors and four male elders. We sing a few praise songs as a congregation. Following that, one of the pastors prays using exclusively masculine language. The sermon is not a sermon at all and is labeled "teaching" instead of "preaching." In 35 minutes of teaching I cannot remember being challenged or inspired to do anything.

My eyes fill with tears of sadness as I realize that this service is not very worshipful for me. I find myself asking: *What am I doing here? This is not home to me. Why have I chosen to exile myself from my community of faith?*

My parents and I drive up to Sedona after church and visit the Roman Catholic Chapel of the Holy Cross in the red mountains outside of town. It is absolutely gorgeous. This time I find my eyes filling with tears out of joy and comfort. It is such a holy place, and I feel God's presence there.

On a bronze plaque outside the church is the story of its construction. Sculptor Marguerite Brunswig Staude wrote: "When we consider that just as the soul inhabits a human frame, and the house is built to shelter that frame, it is the mission of the church to shelter and inspire both soul and body. It therefore should not only be a monument to faith, but a spiritual fortress so charged with God that it spurs man's spirit godward!"

Again, I weep because that's exactly how I feel. The church is a holy place to inspire both soul and body. And, try as I might, a gym or an antiseptic auditorium does not send my spirit Godward. First Church has such a beautiful Norman Gothic style sanctuary. It is God's house and it causes my spirit to soar. I am truly grateful that I can worship there week after week. On the other hand, I don't mean to imply that God cannot and does not appear in the most ordinary of places. God is present wherever hearts, minds and eyes are open to receiving him.

In the afternoon, my parents and I go on a Jeep ride in the Coconino National Forest. It is one of the most unique experiences I have ever had! I cannot fathom how the Jeep can go up and down unbelievably steep rock formations. Our guide, Eric, is great. He knows his stuff, is personable and is a fine driver.

At a few stops along the way, we encounter a group driving two Grand Cherokees. It is incredible that these vehicles can go over the rocks the way our Jeep does. We find out they are prototype Jeeps by Chrysler, shipped from Detroit, with engineers flown in to test drive the vehicles for their off-road capabilities. It was determined that Sedona was the best place to test them. Fascinating.

Driving along in the Jeep I realize anew how much I need to be outside in order to be connected with creation and with God. When I am stuck all day at my desk, I lose that connection. But I also recognize how much I need the church, worship, and liturgy to be connected with God. Both nourish my spirit. I have learned, too, that I need people to be connected with God. So far on my renewal leave, I have been inspired by two fishing guides, a Taliesin guide and a Jeep driver. While none of them professed any kind of religious beliefs, all of them displayed the presence of God through their passion for what they did.

* * *

Last night I called Gary to see how Sunday went. Part of me felt very anxious about calling because I knew I would feel guilty about not being there. Sunday mornings are very complicated for people who lead worship. So much has to fit into an hour. If Gary and I don't plan carefully, we risk incurring the wrath of those with 12:15 p.m. brunch reservations. There has to be a good flow to the service with no dead space, yet it can't seem rushed.

The details are endless and I often find myself thinking about them during the service. Did the acolytes light the Christ candle? Is there water in the baptismal font? Are the ushers ready to receive the special offering? Are there enough tenors today to sing the four-part anthem the choir so diligently practiced? Did all the people being received as new members show up? Do the communion servers know where to stand? Did I remember to put my visual aid for the children's time behind the pulpit? Is the sound technician aware of everyone who needs a microphone? Will the layperson doing the special announcement keep to the three-minute limit? Does the organist know we're only going to sing three stanzas of the last hymn? Am I wearing the right color stole? Is there a run in my hose? Are my children here? I don't see them in the balcony. Are they still in my office? Where are they?

Sunday morning is often a blur, so I knew Gary had a tough day. When there's only one of us there, it's even worse. Gary seemed to be upbeat, though. Except for the fact that the projection screen got stuck during worship and there was some chaos surrounding the Homecoming dinner, all went well. God is good.

I feel better but still experience lingering guilt about shirking my responsibilities. Mom said yesterday that some of her friends have been asking how I could possibly leave my children and go away for three months. Good question. It's not easy, but I have the full support of my husband, my three children and my congregation. Otherwise, I couldn't do it.

* * *

Americans will always remember where they were on September 11, 2001. Just as I remember where I was when President Kennedy and Martin Luther King Jr. were assassinated, President Reagan was shot and the space shuttle Challenger blew up, so I will always remember this day. I was in Arizona sitting in a condo with my mother and father.

At 7:20 a.m. I have just come back from an early morning run when my folks tell me what happened. Two airliners have crashed into the World Trade Center towers, a third has crashed into the Pentagon and a fourth has crashed somewhere near Pittsburgh. As I sit there in stunned silence, I see live on television the collapse of the second tower of the World Trade Center. We have no words.

I call Gary and learn that the church is having a prayer service tonight. What a wonderful ministry it will be to the congregation and the city of Grand Rapids. We also talk about how I am going to get home. All flights across the country are canceled until tomorrow at noon, and I am scheduled to leave at 6:50 a.m. I am planning to be home for one day before traveling to France. Gary is very fearful of me flying in the next few days and says I would most likely not get to France on Thursday. I wonder if I will get to Taizé at all now. I broach the subject of renting a car and driving back to Michigan, but Gary advises against it.

I also talk with Talitha. At school, she saw the second plane fly into the World Trade Center live on television. I am so emotional that I start crying when I tell her I will not be able to be at her cross-country meet and school open house the next night. I feel as if I have abandoned everyone. I feel utterly isolated in Arizona while my children and husband need me in Grand Rapids. I apologize profusely to Talitha and she is very gracious about it.

I call my travel agent in Grand Rapids, who puts me on three flights—one on Wednesday afternoon and two on Thursday in case flights do not resume until then. I feel better about getting home, but still have no idea what to do about France.

All day I take my anger and helplessness out on God. *Why God? Why couldn't you have prevented this? What do you think about this, God? Are you happy? How can you sit back and just let this happen? How can we trust you now? What good are you? Why did you create people who are capable of doing such a thing? Why can't people live peaceably with one another?*

I feel so inadequate, not being able to do anything. I know the church is already setting in motion a response to the terrorist attacks. There was a special staff meeting to determine how the church could best minister to the needs of parishioners. People will be coming to First Church for help and comfort who have never been in the church before. There will be prayer meetings and special worship services. Gary will write a completely different sermon and will be working with a seminary intern and youth minister, neither of whom is experienced in leading worship. I am far, far away, unable to help.

My entire renewal leave looks pretty irrelevant in light of what has happened today. I wonder how it will affect the rest of my time away. Since I cannot do anything here, I will simply be in prayer. As evening descends upon Arizona and the world seems to spin out of control, I continue in prayer for all those families who have not heard from their loved ones and are living in pure agony and uncertainty. I can do nothing except hope they know how the entire country mourns for them and their loved ones.

I also think about those who may be trapped in the buildings and have not yet been rescued. I pray they can gather the inner resources to make it through the night knowing that the love of Christ surrounds them even as they live in the midst of hell.

Suddenly, all of the lights in the condo go off. It's 8:23 p.m. *What in the world is going on? Is this connected with the terrorist attacks, or is it a coincidence? Lord, have mercy on us all.*

Mom and Dad brought a flashlight, so at least we can see. We are in utter darkness, literally and figuratively. We decide to take a walk around the resort and discover that all of Phoenix south of us is without power. At 8:49 p.m., the lights come back on. Our theory is that there was a power surge from too many people watching news about the terrorist attacks. The lights go out again 15 minutes later. Eventually, the lights return.

During this time, I am reading the psalms: Psalm 121, Psalm 130 and Psalm 139. I'm thinking about the events of this momentous day and also about my struggle with feeling useless and isolated when I am needed elsewhere. Psalm 127 cut to the core of my being:

> *If God doesn't build the house, we'll end up with hovels. If God doesn't guard the city, the night watchman might as well go home. It's useless to get up early and go to bed late, fretting about your work; for God gives sleep to those he loves.*

Author Marjorie Thompson talks about how the 14-hour workday has almost become a status symbol in our culture. The busier we are, the more important we must be. I confess that I often feel that way. The problem is not the work itself. The problem is the anxiety I feel about the work I do—that it's never enough—and that what I do does not meet my own expectations. I create my own inner turmoil.

As I stew about my inability to help at such an important time, I can't help but think that good will come out of this for me. The good is that I am learning what it is like not to be in control, to be totally out of the loop and not to have the praise and status of always being in the middle of ministry, of basking in the limelight of helping others. I am learning how insignificant I am and how my pride has gotten in the way of my relationship with God. In short, I am learning how to trust.

* * *

I discover that my afternoon flight is canceled as well as my morning flight. At least now I won't have to go to the airport and sit and wait. My travel agent says her computer shows my flight to Paris on Thursday is either canceled or full. All it shows is zeros. This doesn't sound good. At this point, I don't think I can make it to Paris in time to get to Taizé by Sunday. My alternative plan now is to drive to Hilton Head early next week and then go to France sometime in October. Actually, at this moment I am about to scrap my entire renewal leave. I have no passion for it right now. I don't know what I want. But most things are out of my control anyway.

I find myself fighting this leave. I have lost the life I was leading. I am floundering. I don't know why I am here. I must empty myself before God can find me. I need to make room for God. It's especially difficult because at this moment Talitha has her school open house, and I was supposed to be there. Instead, I sit in a condo in Mesa, Arizona, stranded because of the ban on flights. I cannot go anywhere.

I have to cancel my flight to France, hotel in Paris, rail reservation and week in Taizé. I have no idea if and when I can get there and I have no idea what I am going to do next week. What I do know is that I cannot stay at home because then I will allow myself to get sucked into my job, and that would be the end of my renewal leave.

Here's the heart of the matter. I want attention. I want to be the one to lead the prayer service for the terrorist attack. I want to preach the sermon for Homecoming Sunday. I want to be the one to visit the family dealing with a brain tumor. I want to be in on the decisions about determining use of space at First Place. Now I am out of the loop and feel unimportant, as if my life has no significance whatsoever. Do I really have a desire to serve others, or do I want to serve myself? The balance is so difficult because I believe the more I do and the harder I work and the more excellent I can make our ministry, the more lives I can touch in a positive way and the more people I can point to Jesus Christ. But I have gone too far.

Now I have to let it all go in order for God to make me into a new, more balanced person. 2 Corinthians 4:16 says: "So we're not giving up. It may look like things are falling apart on the outside, but on the inside, God is bringing new life every day because of God's grace."

I want God to create new life inside of me, but already I am seeing how I resist and how difficult it is for me to empty myself of any identity except that of a child of God. Writing in *Sojourners* magazine (August, 1981), Henri Nouwen says that our discipline as Christian disciples is not to master anything but to be mastered by the Holy Spirit. Christian discipline means to create space where we can be transformed into the image of Christ. How true that is for me. When I get to Hilton Head, I want to be intentional about spiritual disciplines, but I need to be careful not to let this be just another task, job or challenge that I can accomplish if only I work hard enough or focus well enough.

Please, Holy Spirit, master me.

* * *

Two days after the terrorist attacks, I awake at 5:45 a.m. and call the airlines. My flights have been canceled for today as well, so I call Gary and talk with him for an hour. We discuss how this may be God's way for me to learn how to "be" instead of "do." There is nothing much to do here. Despite my desire to learn how to be, I'm still thinking, *I don't want to be here. I can be on Hilton Head but not here.* It's kind of like going out for recess. It's great when the playground is full of children, but now it's as if everyone has gone inside, while I'm still outside—all alone—and I don't know what to do with myself.

I read more of Henri Nouwen today. Ever since I took a class from Nouwen during my first year at Yale, he has been one of my heroes. In that class, I also met the man who would become my husband. Gary and I were in a small group as part of Nouwen's class, and one of our assignments was to go off to a monastery for a few days. Obviously, we didn't spend the whole time in solitude!

I took that class, "Ministry and Spirituality," when I was 22 years old. Now, I am 46. How could I have ever understood what Nouwen was talking about? I was so young. I had no life experience. I had never felt the pain I feel now as a result of ministering to the needs of others and dealing with heartache in my own family.

Nouwen has always spoken to my heart because of his honesty and vulnerability. He is right when he says that pastors lose our sense of vocation when we let our need for success, visibility and influence dominate our thoughts and actions. "We have to remember Christ, who did not count equality with God something to be grasped, emptied himself, taking the form of a servant" (Philippians 2:1-11). That's what I must do if I am to pursue my vocation with integrity. Perhaps this renewal leave will give me the time I need to be mastered by the spirit.

The truth is that I am resisting what I say I want to do during my leave. I need to spend time in solitude, in my "prayer closet," so to say, but when I do, my nakedness, faults, obsessions and compulsions are exposed. I don't like it! It's as if I am being stripped away. All my support systems are gone, all the strokes are gone and all the adulation is gone. Right now, all that remains is God and me.

As Nouwen says, nothing is romantic about spending time alone with God. It doesn't "accomplish" anything. But through prayer, humans come to embrace all the suffering of the world, just as God embraces the horrific suffering in New York City. I want to enter more deeply into the heart of God.

I'm Sorry

It's the story of my life, my family, my vocation.

My spirit is sliced up into tiny pieces, wrapped in tin foil and thrown off the parade float to appease the masses;

Everyone wants a piece of me.

I'm sorry I'm such a bad mom.

I'm sorry that I can't seem to balance all the demands placed on me.

I'm sorry I'm such a slouch as a pastor.

I'm sorry I couldn't get supper made because of that evening meeting.

I'm sorry I wasn't home to tuck you into bed and left again before you got up in the morning.

I'm sorry I didn't visit you in the hospital, call you when you were sick or send you a card.

I'm sorry I wasn't there for you when you needed me.

I'm sorry I was stuck in Arizona on September 11, unable to do anything except pray.

I'm sorry that I desperately need this time away.

I'm sorry I can't be the person you want me to become, God.

Always saying I'm sorry, but still praying, dreaming, hoping.

I'm not sorry about that.

And God said, "My grace is sufficient for you."

Off the road in Sedona, Arizona.

CHAPTER 3

Transition

STRANDED IN THE desert southwest, it's difficult to keep a positive attitude about this experience. The only comfort is that we have a place to stay and a car to drive. So many millions of people are affected in a myriad of different ways by the terrorist attacks. Fortunately, I do not have to be in any other place right now—the trip to France having been canceled—so I just have to learn to be content where I am, write as I am able and use the spiritual resources I have to keep close to God. I am absolutely convinced that God is using this experience to help me let go and allow the spirit to master me.

On Friday morning, we learn that all of our flights are canceled until at least Monday, so we are lucky to rent one of the last available cars in Phoenix. We are all psychologically ready to leave Arizona. I have some ideas of what we can do in the car. I can get out my laptop and record Mom and Dad's autobiographies. I also have books to read. Dad and I are splitting the driving.

I look at this cross-country excursion as an adventure. I drive the first three hours and thoroughly enjoy the scenery. We go from desert to hills to mountains to plains to occasional buttes and rock outcroppings, all in Arizona. We drive through a few storms, watching them develop far off in the distance. One time, a rainbow begins to form right in front of us—then a double rainbow appears. It's just like an arch under which we are driving. We certainly do have a beautiful country.

We eat dinner at Rip Griffin's Travel Center in Moriarty, New Mexico. What a fascinating place—a true cross-section of America—filled with people I don't normally encounter. The smoking section is four times as large as the nonsmoking section. In the nonsmoking area, we are surrounded by a family with five little children where the father is wearing a white sleeveless undershirt and the woman is missing several teeth. Next to us are four Native Americans who are deaf and use sign language. I see a solitary truck driver, three teenagers, what appears to be a high school Native American girl's sports team and another couple who look to be traveling.

It brings back memories of churches I have served in the past that did not contain as many professionals as First Church. I'm so amazed at the variety of settings in which I've been called to minister and the broad and wonderful spectrum of people who have been in my churches. My ministry certainly has changed and evolved!

The main feature at Rip Griffin's is its Friday night buffet consisting of all fried foods and a 1-pound hamburger for $6.99, which includes fries and coleslaw. They also sell Jalapeño ketchup by the case. It's amazing what you miss when you travel by air.

I have a great day. During our last hour's drive, we are treated to a brilliant lightning show in the east. After driving 560 miles, we stop in Santa Rosa, New Mexico.

* * *

Who would have thought that on Saturday, September 15, I would be sleeping in Santa Rosa, New Mexico? I am supposed to be in Paris, France! As I lay in bed, I think back to the theme of my last sermon, "One does not discover new lands without consenting to lose sight of the shore for a very long time." I said to the congregation, "When we stick close to the shore, it's safe, isn't it? We know exactly where we are and exactly where we are going. And what happens when we lose sight of the shore? We risk, don't we? We enlarge our borders, don't we? We invite chaos, don't we? We force ourselves into deeper dimensions of trust, don't we? But that's the only way we discover new lands."

Now I am being asked to practice what I preach. Initially, I believed that losing sight of the shore meant going off on my renewal leave. I was losing sight of my familiar life—family and church. Now I see that the carefully laid plans for my leave have been like sticking close to the shore. I'm out in deep water at the moment and I don't know which direction to swim. I don't know what I am going to do in the next few days, let alone next week or a month from now. But letting go of the familiar is the only way I am going to enter into communion with God. I think of the words of St. John of the Cross from *The Ascent of Mt. Carmel:*

> *To come to enjoy what you have not*
> *You must go by a way in which you enjoy not.*
> *To come to the knowledge you have not*
> *You must go by a way in which you know not.*
> *To come to the possession you have not*
> *You must go by a way in which you possess not.*
> *To come to be what you are not*
> *You must go by a way in which you are not.*

This morning we travel through New Mexico and Texas on Interstate 40, which is the old Route 66, built in 1926 as one of the first roads from Chicago to the West Coast. We see thousands of cattle along the highway and many oil rigs. What a fascinating country.

We begin the day talking about the terrorist attacks, referring to an article in today's Albuquerque newspaper about Jerry Falwell and Pat Robertson's comments. I had the opportunity to sit next to Jerry Falwell several years ago at the Grand Rapids Rotary Club. He was the speaker and I gave the invocation. I am always amazed and humbled that people I have such deep disagreements with can be charming individuals when I meet them personally.

Falwell blames the September 11 attacks on pagans, abortionists, feminists, homosexuals, the American Civil Liberties Union and the People for the American Way. He says that he points his finger in the face of every group that tries to secularize America, saying, "You helped this happen." Later, he says that God lifts a curtain to allow our enemies to give Americans what we probably deserve. Pat Robertson agrees with Falwell.

Furthermore, Robertson released a statement saying that Americans have insulted God by allowing abortion and "rampant Internet pornography." According to Robertson, our Supreme Court has stuck a finger in God's eye, and our highest government officials have insulted God. Then, Falwell says, we wonder, "Why does this happen?"

I give my parents a lot of credit for seeing right through Falwell and Robertson. They say, "What do abortion and homosexuality have to do with the terrorist attack? Why do they have to blame someone, anyway? Aren't the terrorists responsible for their own actions? It's like blaming the victim, isn't it?" My mother says, "They will rue the day when they said those things." Falwell and Robertson's insensitive statements shock me. The White House calls the remarks "inappropriate." That's being as generous as possible.

It does evoke the age-old question of why such terrible and unimaginable tragedies happen. Many of us feel compelled to come up with an answer when there isn't any answer other than the fact that we humans have the capacity for great evil. We cannot blame God for the choices humans make. The weekend edition of *USA Today* has a brief synopsis of Harold Kushner's book *When Bad Things Happen to Good People*, for which I am grateful. Kushner presents the possibility that perhaps God is not all powerful—that God has given up some of God's power for us to have freedom. God is not to blame when bad things happen. Rather, God weeps with us, offers comfort and consolation and gives us the strength to endure and to be there for others who are suffering.

Another subject of conversation is what we would be doing if we had chosen to stay in Arizona. We agree that the only two questions of the day would have been, "Where shall we play golf?" and "Where shall we eat supper?" We also agree that it isn't much of a life or a vacation.

It reminds me of something said at the funeral of Gary's uncle Porter Raley last summer. The pastor was mentioning how Porter, who was retired, was walking along the beach near Sarasota, Florida, one winter where he and his wife Jean were spending a few months. As Porter walked, he asked himself, "What am I doing here? This is a waste of time. I have more to give than simply walking on the beach."

When they returned home, Porter and Jean enrolled in *Disciple Bible Study*, after which Porter agreed to teach this 34-week intensive study. He also volunteered to be the chairperson of the building committee for the new addition at their church. Porter devoted himself completely to that project, and today it stands as a symbol of his dedication and realization that he had more to give in his life after he retired.

My parents and I then get to talking about pastors—specifically how congregations and pastors work through conflict. I say that I'm glad to be part of a denomination that has a specific committee, the Staff (Pastor) Parish Relations Committee, which has the dual role of both evaluation and support of the pastor. They interpret the ministry of the pastor to the congregation and the needs of the congregation to the pastor. All difficulties are routed through that committee.

We also talk about what the most important qualities are for a pastor to have, knowing that no pastor can be superior at everything. My parents say that it is important for pastors to communicate well, to know the names of their parishioners and to be the kind of person with whom they can talk if they have a problem. What they don't like are pastors who are not friendly and don't seem concerned about parishioners as individuals. We decide that preaching ability may be the most important quality, but relational skills are just as important. My parents, both faithful churchgoers all their lives, say they have had both kinds of pastors: pastors who could preach but had poor relational skills and pastors who were very personable and caring but could not communicate well in the pulpit.

May God help me to demonstrate both of those qualities!

* * *

We finally roll into Grand Rapids at 7:15 p.m. The three extra days I spend with my parents in the car are a precious gift. It finally dawns on me that my parents are in their 70s and are not getting any younger. Although they are still healthy and vital, they are not as fast as they used to be. They can't keep up with my pace, and they are more content than they used to be to sit and read and watch television. I suspect I'll never again have them all to myself for that period of time.

It feels weird to be home. Mom and Dad, Talitha, Gary and I go out for supper before my parents continue the last leg of their journey to Pennsylvania. As we eat, I ask how it went this morning in church—this being the first Sunday after the attack. I ask because I know I should. It's very difficult to hear Gary's response, though, because I keep thinking, *I should have been there. I should have been there. I should have been there.*

I feel totally out of the loop. It's as if all of these important events are happening and I don't matter at all. There is my ego interfering again, my need for attention, my lack of confidence that what I am doing is OK and not just an act of incredible selfishness. I just hope I don't run into anyone from the church. It sounds self-serving, but contact with church members would bring me back into involvement with concerns from which I need to be distant right now.

* * *

Talitha is at school, and Gary is at church. I have a lump in my stomach. I feel so different at home than when I was in Montana and Arizona. The dining room table is piled high with mail to look through, papers to sort and bills to pay. I feel like screaming. *How have I lived this way for so long?*

Where can I find my quiet place? I'm going out for a run. I know that will help. I also did not start the day with devotions, which I have done daily since I began my renewal leave. I could not do it, though, because I had to get some financial matters straightened out before Gary left for the church. But that's how it's always been, isn't it? The demands are not going to go away. The juices are flowing. The adrenaline is kicking in. I feel a compulsion to get these tasks done right now, but I must stop. I cannot let myself do this.

Please God, help me. I have to find a better way to live.

I go out for a run and take time to meander through trails at Manhattan Park that I have never tried in eight years. That's sobering. When I get back, I do something else I haven't done in ages. I take a bath! I am always in such a hurry that I don't give myself permission to take a bath. I can take a shower, dress, dry my shoulder length hair and get out the door in 15 minutes. I never waste time. Now that I have time on my hands, will I use it wisely? Do I even *have* to use it wisely? Can't I just kick back and do nothing? Is it OK to waste time? If I don't, will I come back refreshed and renewed?

Henri Nouwen writes in *The Way of the Heart* that pastors seldom have a time when they don't know what to do. Rather, we go through life continually distracted so that we never pause to rest or consider whether any of the things we think, say or do are worthy of thinking, saying or doing. We just keep on following the "musts" and "oughts" passed on to us, believing that they are the authentic words of the gospel. I doubt I am the only one convicted by those words.

* * *

Numerous times I have heard these words, "Don't become a pastor unless there is absolutely nothing else you feel called to do. It's too difficult." I have also said these same words to others contemplating ministry.

From where does the call to ministry come? I felt called to ministry as a little girl. I was affirmed in everything I did in the church. Zion Mennonite Church was filled with encouragers. It was my spiritual home, and I felt empowered to do all kinds of things.

Is the call only an individual call? I don't think so. Certainly, there has to be a personal call. On the other hand, the confirmation of a call by the community of faith is important, too, because it helps safeguard against people going off the deep end and feeling they are called to pastor when they are entirely unsuited for the ministry. Perhaps their call is to something else.

I am convinced that God calls every person to ministry. All Christians don't have to become pastors to pursue their calling, however. At First Church, we place great emphasis on discovering and using our spiritual gifts. One of my greatest joys is seeing people catch fire for God because they hear God's call and respond through service.

My call is what keeps me going when ministry gets tough. When I think about quitting, I remember that I have never felt called to do anything other than pastoral ministry. Even when I was studying organ and church music in college and graduate school, my call was to pastoral ministry. Fortunately, I am usually able to recognize when I am burned out and need a break. That's how I felt a year and a half ago, and that's why I am on this renewal leave. I knew then that I needed an extended time away from ministry if the second half of my career was going to bear fruit.

I could tell that my spiritual reserves were being depleted. I also admitted that many people in my congregation had a more vital spiritual life than I did. Outwardly, I was fine, but inwardly, I was empty. At First Church we encourage people to take high commitment courses like *Disciple Bible Study*, *Christian Believer* or *Companions in Christ*. I would see these folks grow so much during their year of study, but I would not grow along with them at the same rate. I would not take the time I needed to nurture my spirit because too many other tasks took precedence—like running the church. I would encourage others to deepen their spiritual life whereas I just plowed ahead—doing, doing, doing.

Now I am taking time to reflect and devote to my spiritual life so that I can come back with a different perspective and a willingness to yield to God and allow the Spirit to master me. The spiritual life is not something that I can initiate. It is a gift from God that I can either freely receive or not. In the past I have not chosen to receive it fully. Now I am saying, yes.

I remember Eugene Peterson's words in *Working the Angles* that the three most important parts to pastoral ministry are "a trained attentiveness to God in prayer, in Scripture reading, and in spiritual direction." That's how ministry gains integrity.

Lord, I want and need to be more attentive to my spirit and God's spirit. I yield my life to you completely. Mold me as you will. Amen.

* * *

This afternoon I take Tamale, one of our four cats, to the vet. As I am writing a check, one of the receptionists says, "I read in the paper about your leave. Did you already take it?" I reply that I am in the middle of it and should be in France right now. How in the world did she know who I was? Just goes to show, I am always on duty when I am home. Even though I live in a city, I can never be just me. No matter where I am, some-one probably recognizes me and is looking to see if I live what I preach. It's like driving to church. Even if I am in a hurry, I try not to pass anyone for fear I am passing a parishioner who might get upset.

It's been kind of nice so far in this renewal leave. I don't think one person has asked me what I do for a living. I certainly don't volunteer the information because once people know I'm a pastor, they act differently. They are on their best behavior. Actually, it's rather amusing, but I do yearn for times when I can be anonymous.

Last night I called our daughter Sarah. I feel bad that I often call her reluctantly. I am reluctant because I know she will not be in a good mood and it breaks my heart. When I asked how she was, she said she could be better. I guess I have to take that as good. Sarah is lonely. She says she has no friends, has no roommate at the moment and doesn't like her classes. She has not found a job yet, and she dropped one class. She says, "People do it all the time." It is so frustrating trying to talk with her because I am very different from Sarah. Gary and I find ourselves saying the same thing to her over and over and over, but she can't hear it. She is the kind of person who has to learn by herself—usually the hard way.

* * *

After two days at home, I'm on the road again to Hilton Head, South Carolina. I drive straight to Knoxville, Tennessee, only stopping to use the restroom and get gas. The drive today is a revelation to me. At the last minute, I remember there is a CD player in our new car, a Hyundai Elantra. I pick up a bunch of Gary's CDs, saying with great pride, "You know, I don't own any CDs myself. I've never bought a CD in my life."

An hour into the drive, I listen to a CD of choral music by the Mormon Tabernacle Choir. I soon find myself weeping because the music is so lovely. I realize that I have not listened to orchestral, organ or choral music for years. Here I am, with undergraduate and graduate degrees in organ performance, and I no longer have time to listen to music! Yes, that's been my excuse.

As I listen, I remember how much God has spoken to me through music in the past. I feel an overwhelming regret for having forgotten that. I am now so busy that I do not make time to listen to beautiful music unless it's a concert at our church and I am obligated to go.

The next CD is J.S. Bach organ music. Now, I really tear up. The water inside the car flows as does the pouring rain outside. How long has it been since I have listened to a Bach prelude and fugue? And how long has it been since I have played a Bach prelude and fugue? Bach is my all-time favorite composer. I concur wholeheartedly with Pablo Casals, the composer and premier cellist, when he said, "Bach, like nature, is a miracle."

For years, the organ was my life. In 1968, my home church, Zion Mennonite Church, built a brand new facility on the outskirts of Souderton, Pa., because our former building in town was too small. Great care was taken in the design of the church, and we hired Ed Sovik from Minnesota to be our architect. We determined that we wanted a freestanding pipe organ in the new sanctuary and contracted with Charles Fisk of Boston to build it. Zion's tracker action organ is still an outstanding instrument today.

When I was a high school sophomore, I went with my parents to an organ recital by Joan Keller, an organ major in college and the daughter of our associate pastor. I can still remember the awe I felt, especially when she played the music of Bach. I was familiar with organ music and classical music, so what I heard wasn't new. However, there was a stirring inside of me that wouldn't go away. That stirring only intensified when Joan was killed in a car accident shortly before her college graduation. It was a deeply tragic time in the life of our congregation. It was the first funeral I remember attending.

That summer I asked my father if I could take organ lessons. He was delighted because he had been asking me that question for several years. At the beginning of my junior year, I started taking lessons in a nearby town from an organist who was a very fine and demanding teacher. I had an hour lesson: one half was performance, and the other half was counterpoint. I found my niche. Because I was so active in sports and other school and church activities, the only time I could regularly practice was at 5:30 a.m. I would drive to the church by myself in the pitch dark, unlock an empty building and practice until 7 a.m., when I'd drive home and get ready for school.

After high school, I attended Wittenberg University and majored in organ. From there, I went to the Yale University School of Music and Institute of Sacred Music and earned a master of music degree in organ performance. For many years, I spent hours a day practicing. Now, I don't even listen to organ music, let alone play the organ.

Sheer pleasure.

Those are the words that best describe my feelings while listening to classical music in the car today.

Frankly, I am stunned by my intense reaction to the music. It is totally unexpected and leads to further reflection. I see how I began to neglect other loves in my life, and I weep over what I missed. I have missed music deeply, both listening to and performing choral and organ music.

But that's not all. I don't go to museums anymore. When I was in college and graduate school, I used to love to visit art museums, especially in Europe. Now, I have no time for such "idle pleasures."

I used to take a lot of pictures. Years ago, however, I gave up picture-taking, saying it was too much trouble putting them into albums. I'm glad Gary convinced me to take a camera to Montana and Arizona because I have wonderful pictures that I will treasure for years to come.

Music, museums, picture-taking—they're all symptomatic of my neglect of the spirit. In the past, they have fed my spirit and brought joy to my life. But, in recent years, I've had no time for any of it. Another example of how I resist what I need to do to nurture my spiritual life.

Now that I am at recess, I am beginning to feel all sorts of stirrings in my spirit. I am remembering activities I used to love but have shut out of my life and also beginning to acknowledge that now is the time to make the necessary changes in my life so I can regain those loves. I realize in the car that I even forgot to bring my tennis racket to Hilton Head. I used to love to play tennis, and now I'll have some time. Who knows? I might find someone with whom to play.

Yesterday, I called a good friend and began talking about everything I had to do before leaving for Hilton Head. I mentioned it brought back memories of how strung out I was before I left on my renewal leave. I said I didn't think I could live this way anymore. She said, "It sounds as if you're addicted." My mouth dropped open, but I was too surprised to say anything.

Yes, I admit I'm work-obsesed, and I find it almost impossible to relax. But the truth is that, yes, I am most likely addicted to work and I cannot give it a rest. I know from contact with Alcoholics Anonymous that addiction cannot be dealt with until we submit and let go to a higher power.

There's that statement again. Developing a spiritual life is not something we can master. We must allow the Spirit to master us.

It reminds me of a quote from poet and essayist Adrienne Rich, which I have kept in my Day-Timer for years: "When someone tells me a piece of the truth which has been withheld from me, and which I needed in order to see my life more clearly, it may bring acute pain, but it can also flood me with a cold, sea-sharp wash of relief."

* * *

The journey to Hilton Head isn't all tears. I have a good laugh as I drive past the site of one of my most embarrassing moments ever. Two staff members and I were coming back from a conference in Ohio. We were meeting with pastors and staff of downtown urban churches in the Midwest to network and share issues of common concern.

We had to leave the conference early because I had to officiate at a 6 p.m. funeral in Grand Rapids. I completed the funeral sermon before I left because I knew I would get home just in time to change my clothes and get to the funeral on time.

We were aware that we had to get gas, but when we stopped for lunch, we all forgot. My friend drove the van after lunch while I worked on the funeral service and went over my sermon. I was completely oblivious to my surroundings, even after I heard a few chugs from the van. She asked if I knew what it was, and I said no. We went on our merry way until it was too late.

Right past Ann Arbor, Michigan, two hours from home, we ran out of gas on the highway. This was before cell phones. She pulled over to the side of the road directly opposite a rest area on the other side. We decided it would be too risky to try to limp along to the next exit because if we stopped, we wouldn't be near a phone—then we'd be in worse trouble.

I ran across six lanes of highway traffic to get to the rest area. I was pretty panicked because I had not allotted much extra time. In my usual, hurried way, I had planned to get home, change and leave for the funeral. I called AAA and explained where I was and that I was in a hurry because I had to officiate at a funeral two hours away. I'm sure they didn't believe me. I ran back across six lanes of highway to the van, and there we sat for what seemed like hours. I kept looking at my watch, knowing that if I did not show up for the funeral, I'd be in big trouble. In the worst-case scenario, I thought Gary could get into my computer, print off a copy of the funeral sermon and show up instead of me.

A man finally came with enough gas to get us to the next exit, where we filled up and made a beeline for home. I walked into the funeral home at three minutes before 6 p.m., took a minute to compose myself and went on with the funeral as if everything was according to plan. Every time I pass that rest stop, I say a little thank you to God for helping me get to that funeral on time.

* * *

I am eager to get to Hilton Head and begin my time of reflection and spiritual discipline. This is the meat and potatoes of my renewal leave. It's a time to rest, read and write. I hope to meet Jesus more fully during this time and be more attentive to Christ who calls, sends and sustains me in ministry.

I also want to rediscover who I am and who I can be—but who am I, actually? Author Flora Wuellner said that when we are healed and become whole we can see things we failed to see before. We can understand feelings that we previously repressed. We are aware of judgments we made during times of insensitivity. Our words and actions are no longer blinded by ego, and we see relationships in a new light. As we awake, hope dawns, and we claim the power of Christ living in us.

Swim With Me

I don't want to lose sight of the shore, God.

I'm scared that I won't be able to find my way back.

Frankly, God, I've never done transitions well.

I'd much rather stay in my comfort zone than discover new lands.

So why am I putting myself through this?

Why do you put me through this?

I want to stick close to shore.

Keep my feet on the ground and my head above water.

What do I need to learn about you, God—and about myself?

The disciples put their nets out into deep water when you asked.

They couldn't even gather in all the fish.

I'm afraid of losing control—of letting go—of trusting you totally.

Maybe you'll just have to push me into the water, God.

Just don't leave me, please.

Swim with me.

Keep my head above water.

Flood me with a cold, sea-sharp wash of relief so that I can see my life more clearly.

Road trip back to Michigan after 9/11.

CHAPTER 4

Freedom

I ARRIVE IN Hilton Head in mid-afternoon. After finding my condo and setting up the computer, I go for a run. I don't know where I am going, but as soon as I start running, my feet lead me to the most natural place: the beach. I have always felt drawn to the water—perhaps because when I was a child our family spent a week every summer at the New Jersey shore. My spirit never fails to be renewed when I am along the ocean or Lake Michigan.

After a two-mile run to the beach, I begin to walk. High tide had been earlier in the afternoon, and the water is receding. I am astonished to see hundreds of shells! I've been to Hilton Head before, but never have I seen shells like this: whelks, nauticas, cockles, scallops, olives, augers and coquinas. They are small, but beautiful!

I spend a good 40 minutes picking up shells and wandering the beach. Then I panic. *Now just how long do I have? It will take me 20 minutes to jog back to the condo.* Finally, it dawns on me—*I am free.*

I am free!
I am free!

I have nothing and no one to go back to. This is the first time in many, many years that I am absolutely free. I begin to pray out loud:

Thank you God, for giving me this opportunity to be here. I give my life to you right now. I am open to wherever you lead me. Mold me into the person you want me to be.

Later on, as I examine the shells, I am reminded of an article in the *Utne Reader* about the Japanese concept of *wabi-sabi*. Robyn Griggs Lawrence writes that *wabi-sabi* emerged in the 15th century as an alternative to the lavishness of rich ornamentation in Japanese art and culture. It is the art of discovering beauty in imperfection, loveliness in earthiness and authenticity in the ordinary. There is no word in English to describe *wabi-sabi*. The concept is almost impossible for the Japanese to explain to Westerners.

To discover *wabi-sabi* is to see beauty in something that at first glance may seem ugly, dismal or imperfect. It is to see wholeness in objects that are modest, humble and incomplete. As I look for shells, I find myself picking up only the perfect ones at first. That's what most shell-seekers do. As I look further, I realize that the broken, imperfect shells also have beauty to them.

One shell has a bunch of other shells embedded on its back. It reminds me of how I look when I try to carry the burdens and cares of my congregation on my shoulders.

Another shell has its top lopped off. That's me running around like a chicken with its head cut off—harried to the limit by one task after another.

Yet another shell has a hole in its side. I know what it feels like to have my heart broken when relationships fail, children get into trouble and grief over a parishioner's tragic death eats away at my spirit. Just like most of the shells on the beach, I, too, am imperfect: *wabi-sabi*. I am not all that I could be, and I am not yet what God has made me to be. Yet I am still beautiful, a child of God.

Shortly before I left for my renewal leave, two people suggested that I read *Gift from the Sea* by Anne Morrow Lindbergh. In an effort to search out good books, I constantly ask people what they are reading. If more than one person recommends the same book, I take it as a sign from God that I must read it too. I went down to the basement and found *Gift from the Sea*. I had written inside the front cover, "Laurie Hartzel, Christmas 1976."

I received this book 25 years ago as a gift. It was several months after I started graduate school at Yale University. Using the example of shells found along the beach, Lindbergh talks about the need for solitude, the importance of change in relationships and about how, in the midst of so much busyness, we need to discover who we truly are. As I reread the book, I am profoundly touched and amazed at how relevant it still is today—46 years after it was first published. I try to imagine reading the book at age 22 but find myself thinking there is no way I would have gotten this back then. At that time, I didn't have enough life experience to even have a clue what she was talking about.

This afternoon I send an email to a friend:

> *Thanks so much for the email. I got it when I arrived on Hilton Head this afternoon. It is very important for me to know that people are remembering me in prayer. It's just about killing me to be totally out of the loop with how things are going at the church, and Sunday mornings are just awful! I've had a tough time so far with this renewal leave, largely due to my isolation last week when the terrorist attack occurred, then my difficulty in getting home and canceling the trip to France. But I am coming to see how God is teaching me difficult lessons about letting go.*

I am beginning to confront some painful truths about my personality, my workaholic nature and my relationship with God, things I have found easy to repress over the years because I've made myself so busy. With nothing to do, I now feel naked and totally exposed, which is good. One of the most helpful quotes I've come across has come from Henri Nouwen where he says that our discipline as Christian disciples is not to master anything but to be mastered by the Holy Spirit. Christian discipline means to create space where we can be transformed into the image of Christ. In these next weeks of solitude I hope not to try to master anything but to allow God to transform me. It's hard but necessary work if I am going to last in the ministry without self-destructing. I covet your prayers. I have found myself thinking about you a lot over these last few days, thanking God for your friendship, your Christian example and your steadying influence.

Love, Laurie

* * *

Walter J. Burghardt, S.J., says that contemplation is an essential way of entering into reality for a Christian. He writes about taking "a long, loving look at something" whether it is a child, a beautifully prepared meal or a glass of wine. When we take a long, loving look or admire something or someone, it becomes an act of contemplation. I'd never thought of it that way. Burghardt goes on to say that we achieve this level of contemplation by:

- Some sort of desert experience of solitude that interrupts our ordinary life.
- Developing a feeling for festivity—enjoying an activity for itself and not tied to goals.

- A sense of play and wonder, letting your imagination loose with ideas.
- Not trying to possess the object of your delight.
- Making friends with remarkable men and women.

How do I measure up? The second and third points are very difficult for me—especially enjoying an activity for itself, not tied to any goals. That's how I feel about this renewal leave. If I do not produce anything, can I justify the expenditure of time and energy? I do want to enjoy this time, but I am also compelled to put my life and thoughts down on paper so that perhaps I can be a catalyst for others to know and experience the love of Christ.

As I run along the beach this morning, I try to take a long, loving look at creation, and my entire being is filled with joy—pure, intense joy. I think a lot about joy and happiness. Perhaps it's because I have a friend who delights in asking, "Are you happy?" I confess that much of the time I cannot tell her that I am happy. During the past years, I have felt burdened by family concerns and the demands of being a pastor.

My standard reply to her question has been, "I may not be happy at the moment, but I am filled with joy, and that is what matters most." I believe that happiness is directly related to the circumstances of our lives, whereas joy is a deep feeling of peace, love and serenity, which can only come from God and transcends anything that can happen to us. I am not always happy, but I have never yet lost my joy.

* * *

Why am I such a stick in the mud? There is so much to do around here, but I am not enticed. I go to Harbour Town tonight and walk around for a little while but find nothing of interest. After receiving an email from a friend, who pointedly wrote, "SO, WHAT ARE YOU DOING FOR FUN?" I finally rent two videos, *Miss Congeniality* and *Finding Forrester*. Hopefully, they can lighten me up a bit. I have become focused on serious activities like reading and writing. *Why can't I enjoy myself a little?*

* * *

This morning I attend a United Methodist Church. It's wonderful to be in community again, even if it is not my own faith community. I feel very comfortable with worship, despite some differences. The pastor delivers a fine sermon about the terrorist attacks. He is very clear and direct, using Psalm 4:4 as his sermon text: "Be angry and do not sin."

He says that what happened last week was not the culmination of some vast plan of God's retribution but rather was human evil. God's heart was the first to break; God's tears were the first to be shed. He goes on to say that it's OK to be angry. Anger is neither good nor bad, it just is. What we do with our anger is the key. Retribution and revenge is not God's way, for God is stronger than evil.

He cites a poem by Edwin Markham, entitled "Outwitted," which beautifully illustrates the essence of Christ's love:

> *He drew a circle that shut me out—*
> *Heretic, rebel, a thing to flout.*
> *But Love and I had the wit to win:*
> *We drew a circle that took him in!*

Now that I have been away from active preaching for a while, I've been reflecting on the role of preaching in the Christian faith. I believe that the purpose of preaching is to enable people to be aware of God's constant presence and connect with God's love. We share God's word in such a way that lives are transformed.

Preaching has always been terrifying to me. How dare I presume to get up in front of hundreds of people and proclaim God's word! I cannot do it on my own, so every week I humbly ask God to help me. I am acutely aware of my own inadequacies, yet I also feel called to share God's word. I know that preaching is not about me but about God speaking through me.

I am never worthy to preach. I may have yelled at one of my children that very morning. I may be angry with a parishioner because of something that happened at a meeting. I may feel bitterness toward someone who betrayed me. Yet I stand in front of the congregation week after week knowing that I am preaching to myself as much as to anyone else.

For 20 years, I have felt queasy on the Sundays that I preach. I can't eat. My stomach hurts. Many Sundays I put my robe on 10 minutes before the service and wish I could make a quick exit out the back door. I say, *Lord, I can't do this. This is too much for me. I need you.* And, even though I may not be in top form, and even though I may not be as prepared as I would like to be, my prayer is that at least one life has been touched. That's all that matters to me. One life. If only one person says to me, "Thank you for your message. It spoke to my heart," it's all worthwhile.

In my experience, most people who come to church are very serious about their faith and want to grow in their spiritual lives. They do not lack depth, but they are hungry to know more about the Bible and theology. They don't want just to hear about God, they want an experience of God. They want to know if God is real and active in their lives, and pastors are called to provide the bread they seek.

In the last eight years, more than 200 people at First Church have taken an intensive yearlong Bible study called Disciple. They want to grow. Many folks at First Church have a deeper spiritual life than I do. I stand in awe of them. But if I am to be their leader, I must practice what I preach. I need to get my own act together. If they are willing to give me an hour of their time on Sunday morning, I owe them the very best I can give in worship and preaching

But it's not a one-way street. To receive what God offers, they have to be open to the movement of the Spirit in their hearts. In her book *May I Have This Dance?* author Joyce Rupp says that God's song needs an instrument to give it shape and voice. My calling is to help others recognize that they are God's instruments out of which God's love might continually flow.

* * *

I feel today as if I might like to take a golf lesson. I hesitate because I know the instructor will try to take apart my swing and put it back together in one hour. After that I'll get on to the golf course and won't be able to hit the ball for a month because the instructor has tinkered with what little ability I had in the first place. I won't take a lesson unless I really want to take the time to rebuild my swing. My golf game usually gets worse before it gets better.

It's the same with my inner life. Right now I am in the process of taking apart and rebuilding my spiritual life. That means things will get worse before they get better. There are no magic solutions. Years and years of ingrained habits do not go away immediately. Developing the spiritual dimension of my life means adopting new life patterns. It also means hard work, but that's what I am about these days. Many times, though, I think: *Why am I here? Just go home and go back to your old life. It really wasn't that bad, was it?*

Tonight, I go out for my first bicycle ride. What a marvelous time I have riding along the beach, which is almost deserted because of threatening weather. I see four deer on the way to the beach. Two are fawns. About 15 feet out in the water, I notice a dolphin lazily swimming along with me. I find my first sand dollar, never mind that it breaks in my pocket on the way back. I also pick up some big shells brought in by the coming storm. The sky is filled with mysterious shades of blue, orange and gray. The ocean is calm and peaceful. My soul is free and joyful.

God, thank you for revealing yourself to me in so many ways. Help me to pay attention.

* * *

Gary asked a few days ago over the phone, "Are you lonely?" I answered, "Not really." He replied, "That's what I figured." By saying, "Not really," I qualified my answer. I have always enjoyed solitude. I guess that's part of what it means to be an introvert. Normally, I receive energy from being alone. It's being with other people that drains me of energy. I spent long periods of time alone as a child. As a teenager, I would often get up very early before school. If I didn't go to church and practice the organ at 5:30 a.m., I'd take a long walk across the road into the woods and meadows and by the creek. I have never been a party person or one to feel I had to "go out" all the time. I was content to stay home and study or read. For the most part, I was a self-contained person—happy with who I was—not needing the approval of others.

In college, I became a little more gregarious. Still, I would often stay in my room on Friday and Saturday nights, avoiding the parties and studying or listening to music. During my junior year, I had the privilege of studying church music at the Berliner *Kirchenmusikschule* in West Berlin, Germany. The Berlin Church Music School prepared church musicians for service in the state-run Lutheran church, and Wittenberg University offered a junior year abroad in Berlin for organists.

My year in Berlin was, without a doubt, the greatest year of my life. Granted, I had some difficult days in the beginning: having to learn German, cook on my own and leave my entire support system behind. However, I received a first-rate education. I also had opportunities to travel all over Europe, much of the time alone. I appreciated the solitude, but I also remember pangs of loneliness. I felt it when I was looking at a world-renowned painting or seeing a famous site. *Wouldn't it be great to share this with someone?*

When I met Gary, I soon realized he was the one with whom I wanted to share the rest of my life. He was intelligent, sensitive, handsome, a good athlete, a Christian and respected my beliefs. Gary comes from a fine family. I love his parents as my own. He was born and raised in Michigan and graduated from the University of Michigan in Ann Arbor. Gary first enrolled at Yale Divinity School because he hoped to teach at the university level in the area of theology. However, after a field education experience in a nearby church, Gary felt a call to ministry. He is an exceptional pastor, but I know he would have made an equally fine professor.

I thank God every day for bringing Gary into my life. We have numerous common interests and enjoy playing and traveling as well as working together. He is my lover, my best friend and my confidante. Gary has helped me to grow and mature in immeasurable ways. He has always been my greatest supporter and encourager. Yet, one person cannot fulfill our human need for friendship. We humans were meant to live in community, which is something I have preached but have not practiced very well myself.

A big regret in my life is that I never made an effort to stay in touch with high school, college or graduate school friends. My mother still has a group of college friends from all over the country who get together yearly. They've been doing it for more than 50 years! Other than exchanging Christmas cards, I have no direct contact with former friends—and it's my own fault. Because of my introverted nature, I have not always realized that friends are essential to my well-being. I know now that I was wrong.

When I became a pastor, I already had one child, with two more soon to come. I hardly had time to take care of my husband, children and church, let alone cultivate friendships. My first years in ministry, therefore, were devoid of friendships. I also listened to the continual admonitions about pastors not making friends with their parishioners. "Keep your distance," I was told. "Don't get too close."

That was fine for 10 years. Then, I began to feel stirrings inside, a desire for intimacy with other women. I looked about and saw women who had entire networks of other women friends. Their support system was wonderful, but I had nothing. My first venture with friendship involved starting a young women's group at the second church I served. It was good, but I found myself yearning for more.

At my next church, I began pastoring full time and was so stretched that I could not even think about cultivating friends. Again, however, there was a nudging—an ache from within. God sent a woman to me from my church who seemed to want to be friends. I would visit her at her job periodically just to talk. We had the beginnings of a relationship, but I really had no idea how to be a friend to someone, so it was rather awkward. Then we moved to our present church.

It took serious concerns with our daughter Sarah to precipitate growth in my relationships with other women. During that agonizing time, I felt utterly alone. Gary and I had each other, but that wasn't enough. I needed someone to talk to who wasn't so closely involved. I knew I wasn't going to make it through the constant crises unless I had some kind of support system.

By the grace of God, I was given several women who were in the right place at the right time and offered their friendship. I finally said yes. Even though they were church members, I decided these relationships were from God and that I could be friends with them without compromising my role as pastor. Because of my friendships, I have grown and matured in my faith far beyond what I could have ever imagined.

* * *

It's strange, but my very predictable lifestyle here in South Carolina is a comfort to me. I usually wake up around 7 a.m. I spend an hour to two on devotions and then go out for a run. After that, I write for most of the day, taking breaks to do errands, ride my bike or read a novel. Later, I make a simple dinner; I write some more and do my intellectual reading for the day. When I am tired, I go to bed. It's routine, but that's what I crave right now since my life at home is never predictable.

Even though it can be draining, I do thrive on the unexpected things that happen every day in the life of a pastor. Some are annoying, some are tragic and some are just funny. Dealing with these situations usually demands skills I never learned in seminary. Take the story of Muffin, for instance.

Several years ago I was aware that one of our parishioners was experiencing severe depression. She was grieving deeply over the death the year before of her mother, for whom she had sole responsibility since they lived in the same town. Amy was a very attractive, active, single woman in her 50s with no family. At the time of her depression, Amy was under the care of both a doctor and a psychiatrist and had even taken a medical leave from work. Amy and I met occasionally and talked about what she was feeling, but I could see she was getting worse.

It was over a holiday weekend. Amy's best friend, the one Amy leaned on while in this fragile state, was going away for a few days. Amy was feeling alone and scared. I tried to maintain regular phone contact and went over to her house late one night the week before because she didn't want to be alone. I stayed with her for a while and then drove her over to her friend's house to sleep.

I called Amy several times on Friday, but Saturday was a very busy day. I had just finished a wedding when I received a message to call home right away. Amy had committed suicide, and I needed to get over to her house as quickly as I could because Gary didn't have a car. I confess this was one of the few times I ever swore, and in church of all places!

I arrived just as the paramedics were leaving. I was the one to identify Amy, who had simply turned on her car and closed the garage door. She was lying in the back seat, looking very peaceful and holding a teddy bear. I stayed for several hours while the police and medical examiner came. I had never dealt with a suicide before, so this was a difficult experience for me. I tried my best to minister to Amy, but her despair was so great she simply saw no hope.

There was another problem. Amy had a cat named Muffin. In a letter Amy left for me, she asked if I would find a new home for Muffin. I did take Muffin with me that night. However, it took the medical examiner and me at least 15 minutes to locate Muffin in the house and get her into the cat carrier. I found myself crawling under a bed in my suit, hose and high heels trying to capture Muffin!

Amy was clear that Muffin was not to be in a house with children or other cats. Since our family had three children and three cats, that ruled us out! However, Muffin stayed in our home—causing a great deal of anguish for our other cats and me, who had to clean up her messes—until we could find a permanent home for her.

The Muffin case may be extreme. However, I often find myself thrust into situations where my pastoral training is totally inadequate to the task at hand:

- A parishioner is angry and jealous because I gave her husband a hug after worship on Christmas Eve. I give hugs to everybody after worship.

- I am invited to go through the clothes of a person in the church who has died and pick out any outfits I would like to keep.

- A young person comes into my office and tells me he is gay. He wonders if he is still welcome in the church.

- Several teenagers ask if they can put class rings and jewelry in the casket of their friend, who has tragically died.

- One of my children escapes from the church nursery, runs down the center aisle during the offertory on Easter and jumps right into my lap.

- A teenager has been killed in a car accident in the middle of the night, and I must go to the house and inform his mother.

- I am responsible for locating and turning off more than 50 light switches in the church after youth group activities on Sunday night because I'm the last one out of the building.
- I have to search the neighborhood around the church at night for two teenagers who have run away during youth group.
- A parishioner is taken to the hospital by ambulance. I go to the hospital while Gary brings the parishioners' children home and entertains them for several hours.
- I'm playing golf on my day off, and someone in our foursome asks me what I do. I hesitate answering because I really don't want to do any counseling that day, and I don't want to inhibit their language!
- Wearing jeans, I secretly sneak into the office for a few minutes on my day off. Unexpectedly, someone drops in to see me about a very important matter.
- I receive a frantic call on a Saturday afternoon from a complete stranger who says that he is getting married *right now* but the magistrate didn't show up. He forgot and went fishing. The stranger asks if I could do the wedding. I'm glad to help. The only problem is: the wedding is on a boat, it's a windy day, and I always get seasick on boats! It all works out fine.

In retrospect, the Muffin case was really quite simple. We needed to take care of her until a good home was found. The other situations, however, call for a mixture of tolerance, grace, humor, wisdom, compassion, guidance and humility. Before Muffin came along, I naively thought that after 16 years of ministry, I would have seen it all and that nothing would surprise me.

I was wrong.

Come Out and Play

"Come out and play," my childhood self pleads.

Don't you remember?

May I, God? Is it possible to let go of my burdens for a time?

Am I so arrogant that I don't trust you enough to hold them for me?

Delicious freedom—like a butterfly flitting daintily around my head;

Carefree. Let you be in charge, God.

I take a long loving look at my life and think wabi-sabi.

I am so imperfect, obsessed, addicted, unsure of myself,

Yet you created me.

There is no one else like me, thank you, God.

To see beauty in ugliness, perfection in a flawed personality, wonder in hopelessness;

That's grace. That's the call. That's freedom.

"Come out and play," the butterfly teases.

I am released from all that holds me back.

I think I will. Wabi-sabi.

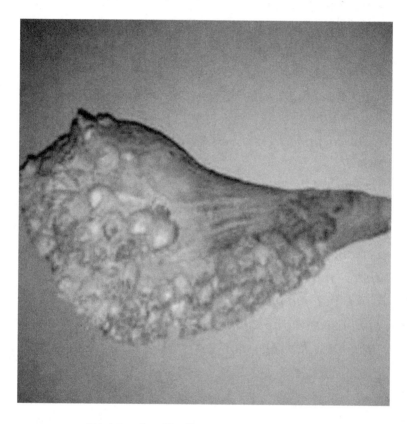

Wabi-sabi: Shell-encrusted whelk.

CHAPTER 5

Seeing and Listening

"**GOD IS MY** light and my salvation; whom shall I fear?"
(Psalm 27:1) I have been overcome and at times immobilized
by fear during my renewal leave. The anxiety began before
I even left. To put it simply, I was afraid of the unknown. I
didn't know exactly what would happen during this time apart,
and that made me uneasy.

Even before the trip to Taizé, France was canceled because
of the terrorist attacks, I felt an unnatural fear about going
abroad. I have to confess that I was not altogether sad when I
had to postpone the trip. I felt I was not ready. I was worried
about the language barrier because, although I have studied
Spanish and German, I don't know any French. I was also concerned about how to get from the airport to my hotel in Paris
and make my train connection to Taizé.

It is difficult to understand my fears. After all, I lived in
Europe for a year and often traveled alone. I have always been
confident and self-assured. Why am I being so skittish now?
The fears continue here at Hilton Head. I have been afraid of

playing golf with another group, fearful that I will get nervous and not be able to hit the ball at all, thus embarrassing myself.

I have hesitated in purchasing tickets for a play, wondering if I'll be able to make my way back to the condo late at night. More than once, I've checked in closets and under beds at night to make sure no one else is in the condo. I check, double-check and triple-check that I have my keys before leaving.

Last night, I finally acknowledged my fears to God. Before, I felt I could make the fears go away by not admitting them. As I laid all my fears before the Lord, it became clear that the heart of my anxiety is a lack of trust. I don't trust myself and my own capabilities. Nor do I trust that God will take care of me.

I am reminded of the story of the rich young ruler who wants to know what he has to do to inherit eternal life (Mark 10:17-22). Jesus says, "You know what do to. You need to keep all the commandments of the law."

The young man says, "I've done all that."

Then Jesus looks at him with love and says, "One thing you lack. Go, sell what you own and give the money to the poor."

The young man goes away grieving, for he has many possessions.

What is the one thing I lack? I can imagine Jesus looking at me with love and saying, "Laurie, what you lack is trust. You find it very difficult to let go of control, to surrender yourself completely to God. Here's the hard part for you. Gaining what you lack does not mean doing anything. You can't fix it yourself. You have to let go, receive the gift and allow my Spirit to master you."

Lord, release me from my fears. Allow me to let go of all that prevents complete trust in your promises.

* * *

Today, I play golf with three older men, Lou, Ken and Frank. Was I really scared before? I play one of my best rounds ever. Golf is one of the great loves of my life. It certainly is the most intellectually challenging sport in which I have ever participated. If I had learned golf as a child I might not get so frustrated today. My problem is that I cannot get my body to do what my mind tells it to do, resulting in shanks, slices, pulls, duck hooks, chili dips, skulls and hitting it fat or thin. With other sports, there seems to be a connection between the level of fitness and athletic success. With golf, however, 95 percent of the game is mental.

I've discovered that when I am stressed, tired, preoccupied or worried, I will play poorly. Conversely, when I put all those distractions aside and focus intently on golf, I also play poorly. The key is to relax, which is bad news for me because I hardly ever relax.

I've concluded that I do not have the right personality for golf. I am a "Type A" person, high strung, a perfectionist, someone who is always seeking a challenge. If I approach golf as a challenge to be met, I will never win. I also don't have time to become the kind of golfer I'd like, so I have two choices. Either I quit playing golf altogether, or I learn to enjoy a game at which I am, at best, average.

I have to learn to cherish the opportunity to be outside and enjoy the ability to play—even if I don't improve. Yes, I have thrown clubs in the past. And yes, I threw a club only a month ago. But I've been much better the past two years. Now that I am relaxed and do not have the stress of active pastoring, my game has improved greatly.

I remember back to our first day of fly fishing. As we were getting our rods ready, Dad mentioned that golf had supplanted fishing as his number one passion. Our guide, John, replied that golf is an evil game because it seduces you. You hit one good shot, and you think you can do it all the time. Later, on the river, I remarked to John that fishing is an evil game because it also seduces you. What brings you back is the big one that got away. Golf keeps me humble. I like to think that's why I keep coming back.

* * *

The leader of our mission trip to Rwanda sent an email last night saying that the State Department had issued a warning against travel in the area of Rwanda where we will be. I don't think it had as much to do with the recent terrorist attacks as with rebel insurgency within Rwanda itself. Dale said he was reluctant to take a group under these conditions and wanted to know what I thought. I call Dale tonight and we agree that, especially with the world on edge because of terrorism, we should not risk going. It is not critical for us to go right now, so we decide to postpone the trip until June 2002.

I am convinced this is the right decision because I was feeling uncomfortable myself. So now what do I do? Plans for my renewal leave have already been changed once. Surprisingly, I am at peace with this new twist. After the past several weeks, nothing surprises me anymore. I am determined to go with the flow, seeking God's guidance about how I should spend the rest of my time.

I call Gary tonight and ask if he wants to spend a week in Paris with me in November. When I was home last week, we talked about how Gary could not find time to visit me in Hilton Head—but wouldn't it be splendid if he could join me in Paris? He's never been there before and is excited about the possibility. I would meet him after my week in Taizé and we would fly back home together. We decide that he might be able to take a Sunday off in mid-November.

* * *

Today is my son's 18th birthday! As I remind Garth in an email this morning, this is the first birthday he has been away from home. He is a freshman at the University of Michigan. The word Gary and I have always used to describe Garth is "sweet." Garth is sandwiched between our two girls—Sarah (the whirlwind) and Talitha (the hurricane). That's been good for us because, in our experience, boys are much easier to raise than girls. It's given us some breathing space!

Even before Garth was born, I could sense his personality. The pregnancy was easy compared to the other two and I was able to jog up to and including the day of his birth. I ran (well, lumbered or shuffled) four miles that morning. The labor and delivery went smoothly and two days later I wrote a reflection on his birth, including the understatement of all time, "He seems like he will be easier to handle than Sarah."

Garth has always had a laid-back personality. He is secure in who he is and pretty self-contained. Garth is responsible, and I have always trusted his judgment. However, he was also accident-prone as a child. We had him at the doctor's office or in the emergency room every few months for everything from putting his finger into an electrical socket, to falling off the jungle gym at the babysitter's, to severely cutting his leg on a broken pop bottle, to crashing his bicycle, to having surgery to remove a stone in his head from a fall, to breaking his arm playing touch football.

Garth has a mischievous side to him. He will play sly jokes on others and can be the life of the party if he chooses. Garth has always been quick athletically. He's small and wiry and was an outstanding soccer player in high school. Garth also has a quick mind. He is very intelligent but doesn't work as hard as he could. He did almost no homework in high school yet had very good grades. He is a computer geek and spends hours in front of the monitor.

When Garth was tested for kindergarten, his teacher asked what his father did. He replied, "He likes to get chocolate at Christmas!" She didn't give up, though. She then asked Garth to connect dots on a page. When he was finished, she was astonished and said no one had ever done it that way before. She declared, "Garth is going to be an engineer!" Now, sweet Garth is in the engineering school at Michigan, and I hope he has a great birthday!

* * *

I think I am finally slowing down. At home I would have 50 things on my to-do list every day. I would hop out of bed between 5:15 a.m. and 6:15 a.m. within seconds of the alarm going off. I would then literally be on the run until 10 p.m. when I would fall into bed utterly exhausted. I fit so many appointments into my day that I would always fall behind and not leave myself enough time to get from one place to another. I was juggling five tasks at once and didn't give anything my full attention.

That has changed at Hilton Head. I get up whenever I wake up. The routine of the day contains very little: running, biking, writing and reading. I rarely go out. I actually read the newspaper every day. I get groceries once a week. I don't feel a need to do anything more—yet still, I am tired. I think I am going to need all three months to truly rest.

The slower pace has allowed me to pay attention to much that escaped me in the past. I see birds everywhere and try to identify them. I enjoy watching a brown bird, which has taken a liking to the mulch in the backyard and spends hours digging in it. I notice brightly colored butterflies, sometimes in groups of two dozen or more. I see deer almost every day. I actually look at trees, bushes and flowers. I am beginning to see the world around me.

Last year I had LASIK surgery on my eyes. It's a relatively new procedure to correct nearsightedness or farsightedness. My vision had been terrible for years. Without glasses or contacts I was totally lost. Hating glasses and having trouble with my contact lenses, I decided to go through with the surgery. It was one of the best things I've ever done—a true miracle. Today my vision is 20/30. I do not even need reading glasses … yet.

Being *able* to physically see, however, does not guarantee that I *will* see. A friend gave me good advice upon leaving. She said, "Pay attention to what is around you." I believe I am finally getting it. Now I understand that everything around me is the glory of God!

* * *

I have been rediscovering the joy of letting the Bible speak to me personally. For years, I had fallen into the habit of reading Scripture in a professional capacity. I have a sermon to write or a Bible study to lead. I have a confirmation class to teach, or someone asks for Scripture about a certain topic. I'm in the hospital and read Scripture to someone who is dying. Certainly, God speaks to me as I use Scripture in all of those settings. However, to nurture my own spiritual life, I need to read Scripture so that it speaks to me personally. Unfortunately, I have not done that well. I would think it selfish—that I should use that time to make one more nursing home call. Or I would feel Scriptured-out and want to use what little free time I had to get lost in a novel.

I am taking a few hours every day to read and meditate upon Scripture and I feel incredibly blessed because of it. I am particularly fascinated by the practice of Scripture reading called *lectio divina*, which means "holy reading". Over the centuries, the Roman Catholic Benedictine order developed this pattern of reading, mediation and prayer. *Lectio divina* has four parts:

1. *Lectio* (reading): A slow reading of the Scripture passage, listening as if hearing it for the very first time; identifying images that catch the attention.

2. *Meditatio* (meditation): An intense reflection on the passage, focusing on words and phrases through which God may be speaking to us.

3. *Oratio* (prayer): A shift from conversing with self to conversing with God. We share with God the struggles, concerns, questions and joys that the text has evoked in us.

4. *Contemplatio* (contemplation): A time of resting and silence, letting ourselves simply be in God's presence.

I like the phrase ancient Christian writers have used to describe this process: that we are "chewing on Scripture, slowly digesting the words and allowing them to become part of our lives." I used *lectio divina* today with Psalm 23. Like many, I have read and spoken Psalm 23 more than any other biblical text during the course of my life. But never did it speak to me the way it did today:

The Lord is my shepherd.

The Lord is my personal shepherd. God knows me.

I shall not want.

God really will supply everything I need.

He leadeth me beside the still waters.

When I am overwhelmed, weak or totally exhausted, God calms me down.

He maketh me to lie down in green pastures.

God gives me permission to rest, even lying down for three months.

He restoreth my soul.

I cannot restore my broken soul. God not only can but wants to restore my soul.

He leadeth me in paths of righteousness for his name's sake.

I want to be a righteous person, not to bring attention to myself, but to bring glory to God.

Yea, though I walk through the valley of the shadow of death, I will fear no evil, for Thou art with me.

Even when times are the very worst, God is there. I do not have to fear the future because the future is in God's hands.

Thy rod and thy staff, they comfort me.

God's protective arms encircle and hold me, especially when I am feeling weak and vulnerable.

Thou preparest a table before me in the presence of mine enemies.

I can sit right out in the open with enemies all around me and not worry because God sits at my table.

Thou anointest my head with oil.

When I feel so empty that I cannot go on, God brings to me the oil of healing.

My cup runneth over.

God pours abundant water all over me. I will never be thirsty again.

Surely goodness and mercy shall follow me all the days of my life.

I picture goodness and mercy as sheepdogs, faithfully following and protecting me.

And I will dwell in the house of the Lord forever.

I am always with God.

* * *

Tonight I send this email to the staff at church, thinking it might be nice for them to know I am still alive:

Hi, everyone.

I thought I'd give you an update on what I am and am not doing. Right now, I am spending time with God rather than doing things for God. I am reading Scripture, praying, meditating, reading theology and novels, reflecting, writing, running, biking and walking. What I am not doing is getting up to an alarm, wearing panty hose, heels, dresses and suits, pretending I'm an extrovert, making lists and running around like a crazy person.

I am spending almost all of my time at my parents'
condo, which has a beautiful view overlooking a
golf course that is way too expensive for me to play.
I went to a United Methodist church on Septem-
ber 23 and an Episcopal church yesterday (I really
needed communion and couldn't wait till next Sun-
day!). Both were wonderful. Tomorrow night I am
going to hear the Hilton Head Orchestra, which is
my big excursion for the week. I pray for each one
of you individually every day and trust that the
fall is going smoothly. I know that my leave-taking
has caused extra work and, most likely, occasional
or frequent hassles for you. Please know that I am
deeply grateful for the opportunity I have right now.
Love to all, Laurie

* * *

I make prayer a lot more difficult than it really is. Prayer is
nothing more than opening ourselves to a God who is always
present—a God who is continually ready to engage us. God is
always with us, but we are not always with God. In prayer, we
allow communication between God and us.

Many of us think prayer is only valid when we are kneeling
in front of our bed, formally talking to God for a half hour at
a time. This faulty assumption has been the cause of needless
guilt. Anything that we do in life can be a prayer. We can pray
while walking in God's beautiful creation. We can pray by simply being quiet and allowing God to speak. We can pray while
driving, at school, in the supermarket or at a sporting event.
Doing our very best in our job can be a prayer. Whenever we
become present to God and allow God to work through us, we
are praying.

In his classic book, *The Practice of the Presence of God*,
Brother Lawrence, a lay Carmelite of the 17th century, wrote
that he disciplined himself to become occupied only with

God's presence. He did it by being lovingly aware of God each moment of each day. Brother Lawrence called it "a silent, secret, and nearly unbroken conversation of the soul with God."

I am so grateful for this time away because I am constantly living in the presence of God. I have no other worries, no other obligations, no other distractions and nothing else to do. It's just God and me. What I am learning, however, is that prayer goes far beyond talking and includes listening. After all, if prayer is two-way communication between God and us, we must not forget to allow God to speak. Often, prayer involves no talking at all. It is simply opening ourselves to hearing what God would say. Listening, however, is difficult work.

Much of my ministry involves listening to others. When people come to see me for the first time, I will often say, "Tell me your story." Everyone has a story, and it's difficult to know how to help people if we don't take time to listen to them. Naturally, some people talk more than others. I've had people come to my office and talk for a solid hour without me saying a word. It takes an incredible amount to energy to concentrate that long without being able to make at least a simple reply!

An elderly, blind woman in one of the churches I served was confined to her home. She had infrequent visitors, so whenever I came she went off on long harangues without allowing me a word edgewise. I was pregnant at the time and would get so tired that I occasionally dozed off because I knew she couldn't see that my eyes were closed.

One night, I was on the phone at home when Garth came into the bedroom and stood quietly for a few minutes. Then he got a piece of paper and started writing. When he was done, he handed it to me and walked out of the room. I was still on the phone.

This is what he wrote:

Mom's Conversation

… yeah; uh-huh; OK; yeah; uh-huh; yeah; OK; uh-huh;

… hmm; OK; uh-huh; sure; all right; yeah; uh-huh; sure.

Later, he said, "What kind of conversation is that, Mom? You were on the phone for 15 minutes and didn't even say anything!"

When people are hurting, they don't want to hear pious religious platitudes, weak efforts to defend God or inept arguments to explain tragedy. They especially don't want to hear about others' or my own experiences with suffering. Nor do they want assurances that times will get better someday. They simply want someone to be with them, to hold them, to listen to whatever they have to say and to love them unconditionally.

It's a continual challenge to resist my impulse to talk, fill the void and make everything all right. It is far better to simply listen and be present. In a ministry of presence, words are not important. Thomas Merton once said, "The more words we need, the greater our poverty."

It's the same with prayer. Far more than talk to God, I need to listen to God. Far more than present God with a list of needs, I need to be quiet and hear what God would say to me.

O God, grant me the courage to listen.

* * *

Today I receive a call from a telemarketer. They can find me even in South Carolina! Telemarketers are a pet peeve of mine. They always seem to call during dinner, the one time when our family is together. I have other pet peeves, too, little things that bother me out of proportion to their importance:

- Putting on a new pair of panty hose, only to get a run before I leave the bedroom. Why can't panty hose be made to last?

- Bad grammar. When people use "it's" instead "its" and "your" instead of "you're," it drives me crazy!
- Call-waiting. I feel incredibly guilty when I make a phone call, only to discover they have someone else on another line. I'd much rather get a busy signal than interrupt their conversation.
- Being left-handed in a right-handed world. Last Christmas I was asked to serve punch at a party, but all they had was a right-handed ladle. It wasn't pretty.
- Servers in restaurants who can't add correctly.
- "Stuff" scattered all over the place, especially when it's scattered in my space.
- Baggers who ask, "Paper or plastic?" Don't make me think. Just put it in a bag!
- People who make a commitment, then don't show up.
- People who don't give their best all of the time.

What I admire greatly about Jesus is that he didn't sweat the small stuff. He was concerned about the big issues of life: poverty, oppression, prejudice, intolerance, grace, mercy and love. I want to be like Jesus. I want to see people as Jesus sees them and not get tripped up by petty things.

Robert Louis Stevenson once said that life is a one-way street and we never get a chance to travel it again. The end of life is "to be what we are and to become what we are capable of becoming." Like Stevenson, I have always felt an urgency about life. God has so much in store for me—there is not a moment to lose. There is so much to experience, so many people to serve, so many gifts to use, so much evil to fight. I'm trying to lighten up. I really am. But I'm afraid I may only lighten up after I become what I'm capable of becoming. When that will happen, I'm not sure.

* * *

Today is a "bad hair day." Little things keep thwarting my plans. I wake up numerous times at night and do not feel rested in the morning. I find two big bugs in the living room. As I open the door to usher them outside, in rushes a lizard. After many attempts, I catch the lizard by the tail and remove him as well.

I spend hours in the morning figuring out my credit card bill online, then have to make a myriad of phone calls about repairs to the condo, family health concerns and travel plans for the rest of my renewal leave. By the time I get to the activities I want to do, the day is half gone.

The church also has bad hair days, times when one thing after another goes wrong. I remember one such Sunday. I had a funny feeling about the day as soon as I put on a new pair of panty hose and got a run within five minutes. It was not a good sign. My fears escalated when one of our elementary youth gave the call to worship and the congregation did not quiet themselves for the prelude as they normally do. The laughter and chatting continued defiantly and unabated. Something was different about this Sunday.

As worship began, chaos erupted. During the first hymn, three seventh-grade boys tried to help an acolyte take off his robe because they were going to sing in the youth choir. The problem was, they were all struggling with the robe in the middle of the front aisle. I hoped nobody else noticed.

As the congregation spoke the opening prayer, our director of music motioned frantically for a key. "I need the key! I need the key!" he whispered. Evidently, he forgot the music for the youth anthem, which was coming up next. He found a key to the music room, raced downstairs and returned to accompany the choir with just seconds to spare. What was going to happen next?

It only took a few minutes to find out. Gary began motioning to me across the chancel. It seemed to have something to do with either his microphone or mine. I assumed one of them was not working, but there was nothing I could do about it. I took a deep breath.

The adult choir came down out of the choir loft this morning to sing the anthem with the piano. Something wasn't quite right, though. The women missed an entrance, the tempo was a little off and the choir was tentative. What else can go wrong?

During Gary's sermon, I began to relax. The congregation seemed attentive—that is, until one of the seventh-grade boys in the front pew took the rope off the acolyte robe and began wrapping it around another boy's hands to make handcuffs. Meanwhile, the four boys in the pew right behind them were "bonding." They were playing some kind of game, and several times one of the acolytes' candle lighters fell on the floor. My motherly stares did not affect them in the least.

Then we got to communion. All was going smoothly until one man dropped his bread in my cup of juice and then put his entire hand in the cup to fish the bread out. I was so astonished I had no time to tell him to just take another piece of bread. I felt sick.

Then, I smelled something. Someone didn't take a shower this morning, I groaned. I hoped no one else noticed. Later, I found out there had been a huge mess on the floor of the women's restroom, which a church member graciously cleaned up before others noticed. Was there a connection?

After worship, I breathed a sigh of relief. We made it! Then my heart sank. A bunch of children were running around eating leftover communion bread. The people who normally took care of the bread were sick and their substitutes had not yet arrived. I had no more energy to chase them down.

During our staff meeting on Monday, we laughed about the comedy of errors we had experienced the day before. Then we began to ask: What went wrong? Were we becoming too casual? What happened to the dignity of worship? Do other churches have bad hair days? Could it have been the full moon?

Then, we came to a startling realization. None of us were bothered by our wacky worship. In fact, several said it was one of the best worship experiences we had in a long time. Why? Because our church was alive! The children were involved in worship, the youth sang for the first time in several years, we had a large congregation, Gary's sermon was compelling and we shared the Lord's Supper as the family of God.

In short, the word became flesh that Sunday at First Church. In the midst of our brokenness, symbolized by all of the glitches, Jesus became real in the breaking of bread. As we came forward to receive communion, nothing mattered anymore. The smell, the noises, the restlessness all faded away as we met the living Christ in the sacrament. "The body of Christ, broken for you. The blood of Christ, shed for you." In receiving the gift of love, God took our imperfections and molded us into one body of Christ. We came to church that day in all of our humanness and somehow, by the grace of God, we left transformed. Trust grace, that's what I say. Don't sweat the small stuff. Always trust grace.

* * *

It was a lot easier to leave home knowing I could remain in close email and phone contact with my children. I knew from the beginning that I could take a three-month leave from the church and a leave from household duties, but I could never take a leave from my children. Fortunately, two are away at college, so only Talitha is at home right now.

Being a parent is the most difficult thing I've ever done. Some of my parenting failures during my children's elementary days were spectacular and caused no end of embarrassment for my children.

- Every Tuesday I begged Sarah not to wear her Brownie sash to school because I could never sew her patches on right.
- One time I was helping in Sarah's first-grade classroom and told the children to put the icing on the Christmas cookies *before* putting them in the oven. What a mess!

- I always dreaded Halloween because I could not sew my kids' costumes or come up with anything clever or original.
- Science fair was a nightmare! I am not scientific, creative or artsy. I tried to be out of town every year during science-fair week.
- Roller-skating was very big in elementary school, and I was a good sport. However, one time Sarah persuaded me to play Crack the Whip, and she whipped me around so hard I fell and cracked my wrist instead of the whip. We spent the rest of the night in the emergency room.
- The year I was Talitha's soccer coach, we not only didn't win any games, we didn't even score a goal!

What continues to amaze me about those early years is that my children love me despite my inadequacies. They didn't care if the patches were not lined up correctly or if I flubbed up the Christmas cookies. They didn't care if they had to wear store-bought Care Bear, Thundercat or Alf Halloween costumes or that their science-fair project was pathetic. They thought it was pretty neat that their mother had a cast on her right wrist for six weeks and was a soccer coach. They have always loved me because I am their mother, period. Gary always used to say they loved me unconditionally when they were little but would demand a payback during adolescence. I prefer to believe their love was pure grace.

I did attempt to get my act together when they were teenagers. How else could I have:

- Huddled in the cold, pouring rain watching my son's soccer games?
- Sat on hard gym bleachers listening to yet another band or choir concert?
- Driven several hundred miles each Saturday so my son could play on a traveling soccer team?

- Driven 60 miles to pick up my daughter from a tennis match just so she was not late for her piano lesson?
- Made over 150 trips to the orthodontist?
- Come home from meetings at 9:30 p.m., then spent the next two hours helping with homework?
- Ever agreed to a piano lesson at 7:40 a.m.?
- Fallen into bed night after night utterly exhausted after shuttling children from one activity to another, overseeing homework and refereeing fights?

I did it for love. That's the only explanation that makes any sense. I did it and continue to do it for love. God has entrusted my children to me for such a short time, and it is my vocation to mold them into confident, capable, caring, Christian young adults. Besides, nothing in this world gives me as much pleasure as watching Sarah sing a solo in a school concert, Garth score a goal in soccer or Talitha run in a cross-country meet. They never say anything, but I know they are happy I am there. Oh, we have our arguments and disagreements, but it is always grace that wins out. Pure grace. That's what families are all about.

* * *

Every morning I spend several hours in devotional time with God. It is a luxury I will never have when I return home. I have found it meaningful to memorize Scripture. What a wonderful spiritual resource upon which to draw in time of need, especially when I have no Bible with me.

I have also developed my own breath prayer, which I repeat continuously throughout the day. The breath prayer has been used since ancient times to remind humans of God's constant presence. Ron DelBene, in his book, *The Breath of Life: A Workbook*, says that the breath prayer usually consists of six to eight words that we choose to express our own needs in relationship to God.

First, we imagine God asking us, "What do you want?" We respond from the heart. "I want peace, healing, reconciliation." This becomes the backbone of the prayer. Then we choose an image for God that is particularly meaningful for us, such as "rock," "shepherd," or "savior." Finally, we put the two ideas together and come up with a prayer.

In answer to the question, "What do you want?" I answer, *I want to be whole.* My only desire is to be one with God, to be so in tune with God's intentions that I am a whole, complete person. My image of God is "light" because light implies seeing, brightness and dispelling darkness. Forming them into a breath prayer, I come up with: *Light of the world, lead me to you.* I want to include "world" because I believe that God wants to bring light to all people everywhere, not just me. And I use the phrase "lead me to you," because I believe life is a journey that has its beginning and end in God. The goal of life is not money, success or adulation but rather wholeness, which is becoming one with God.

My breath prayer now goes with me everywhere. It is becoming a part of who I am. How amazing that in 20 years of ministry, I have never formed my own breath prayer or even knew much about it! It's just one more indication of how I have been so caught up in doing for God that I have forgotten how to spend time with God. The countless hours spent doing good deeds have robbed my inner life of its vitality. I can see that clearly now and I have neither desire nor energy to return to that rat race.

Light of the world, lead me to you.

* * *

From as early as I can remember, I have been a leader. As a child, I organized the neighborhood games. In athletics, I was often picked as a team captain. I was president of the National Honor Society. I gave the valedictorian's speech at my high school graduation. I have always felt comfortable being responsible for groups of people.

Being a pastor means being a leader. Gary and I lead a congregation of 900 people as well as two-dozen professional staff. Some say leadership cannot be taught. You either are or aren't a leader. The ability to lead may be innate. However, the ability to be an *effective* leader is a continual process of learning, growth, self-examination and improvement.

As part of this renewal leave I have made a commitment to assess my own ministry, which involves making a list of what I believe are the most important characteristics of a leader.

The primary quality of a leader is vision. The words of Proverbs 29:18 are true. "Where there is no vision, the people perish." First Church wants Gary and me to have a vision of who our congregation is and where we are headed. We have incredibly gifted and visionary laypeople, but they want us to lead the way. That vision can and should be captured in a mission statement, but vision is also articulated by who we are as leaders and not solely by what we do.

Leaders must be willing to risk. Congregations are, by nature, conservative. They are invested in preserving the status quo. However, just as individuals cannot grow without risk, so congregations cannot grow without risk. Growth in spiritual maturity, outreach and vision as well as numbers comes only by dreaming big.

Last year, our congregation was presented with the opportunity to buy a four-story office building and parking lot across the street from the church. For years, we had sought additional parking knowing that our current, inadequate parking was hindering our program and outreach and would severely limit any future ministry. The purchase of this property would more than double our parking. However, what were we going to do with 20,000 square feet of office space?

Gary and I believed God was challenging our congregation: "You want parking? OK. I'll give you parking. But with it comes a building. You figure out how to use it for ministry, and I'll be with you all the way."

We had not yet completed payment on the last renovation to our facility. Three major renovations in 10 years had stretched our congregation's financial capabilities to the limit. Yet, to their credit, our congregation took a tremendous risk, raised the money and bought the property. Why? They believe in our vision to be a downtown church in Grand Rapids committed to minister to all of God's children.

Pastors have to be effective verbal and written communicators. Sunday morning is the one time of the week when we have contact with the most number of members and visitors. If people are willing to give up an hour of their time to come to worship, I owe it to them to prepare the very best sermon I can. I also spend quality time preparing the weekly pastor's column in our newsletter. I see the newsletter as a way in which I can help the congregation get to know who I am, what I do and why I do it.

Pastors have to be savvy administrators. Organizing and managing the life of a congregation is not a glamorous task. It doesn't give a pastor affirmation and enhance self-worth the way preaching and pastoral care does. But I am convinced that a congregation properly organized for ministry and mission can do far more than a church where everything is continually thrown together in a haphazard manner without thought or careful attention.

I just finished a book by Bob Greene called *Duty: A Father, His Son and the Man Who Won the War.* In the process of being with his father during his illness and death, Greene discovers that his father, who served in World War II, idolized Paul Tibbetts, the fighter pilot who dropped the atomic bomb on Hiroshima in August 1945.

The book is a fascinating account of the role duty played in the World War II generation. What especially interested me was how Greene's father described his work as a manager. His job was to "organize, delegate, supervise and check."

That's how I view my role as an administrator in the church. After organizing the life of the congregation, I have to delegate responsibilities to other staff and lay leaders. Together, we set goals and objectives. But that's not all. I have to continually supervise and support those people in their work, then check to see if they have accomplished their goals.

Unlike in fly fishing, follow-through is critical in administration. Attention to detail can make the difference between success and failure. I'm not talking about micromanaging but simply ensuring that tasks are completed in a timely way. No one likes to take time for administration, but it reaps great benefits.

The one addition I would make to this management style is appreciation. We must take time verbally and in writing to express gratitude for what our volunteers and staff accomplish. One way I do that is by writing notes to people. I know how it makes my day when someone jots me a quick note affirming something I have done. I, in turn, try to let people know how much their commitment and dedication means to the church and me. Take time to appreciate!

Good relational skills are critical for pastoral leaders. If you're a pastor and you don't like people, you're going to struggle. In my experience, most church members are not demanding. They're not critical and they're not complainers. All they want is for me to know their name, help them find the right ministry, and be assured that when they have a need, I will be there. The ministry of presence cannot be emphasized enough. It's amazing and humbling, but whenever I walk into a hospital room, people seem to sense comfort and peace, because I represent God. I convey hope, love, grace and forgiveness. I take no credit; it's the One I represent. It's essential for pastors to find ways to be present in times of crisis.

Integrity is an essential quality for pastors. Parishioners want to know if I am real, if I am who I say I am. They need to be able to trust me before they will entrust to me the deepest burdens of their hearts. I need to be honest, open and genuine—not only at church but wherever I am. I am always on duty.

Other professionals can be effective in what they do and not be good role models. Professional basketball player Charles Barkley always insisted that he was not a role model and did not have to act like one. He was still a good basketball player. By most accounts, Bill Clinton was an effective president—although his moral conduct was less than exemplary. Pastors cannot separate personal integrity from their professional duties. Integrity is fundamental to effectiveness in ministry.

A positive attitude is a must. Nobody likes a whiner and no one likes to be around people who are sour, depressed and complain all the time. By contrast, people love to be with those who are positive, cheerful and always have a smile on their face. A pastor is a cheerleader. It's our job to have a "can do" attitude, to continually encourage our parishioners and staff, saying, "We can do this. It's gonna work. It's within our reach. Go for it!"

A pastor needs to be well grounded, emotionally and spiritually. It's common knowledge that some pastors enter the ministry to have their own needs met. Yes, ministry can be very affirming. However, if the focus is on us and not on God and our parishioners, we'll never survive. Our emotional needs must be met through personal relationships with family and friends. Every pastor needs a strong support system, and our spiritual needs must be met through a vital relationship with God. Only then can we minister effectively without letting ourselves get in the way.

Finally, strong pastoral leaders are servant leaders. They must be willing to serve at all costs. As I write this, I'm saying: *Wait a minute. If we give too much, we'll burn out. We have to be careful about limits and boundaries. We can't serve at all costs.* That's true. I've learned that lesson the difficult way. That's a primary reason why I am taking this renewal leave. I still believe, however, that I am a servant. My calling is to love and serve my people. That's all. Love and serve God's people.

How am I doing as a leader? Suffice it to say I am a lot harder on myself than others are. This renewal leave has revealed I have a lot of growing to do—especially in the area of being spiritually grounded. By deepening my own relationship with God, I will be more effective in everything else I am called to do.

Trusting Grace

Your word is a lamp for my feet and a light for my way.

Groping for meaning and direction, I muddle through life,

I am a peregrina, a wandering pilgrim.

I journey with no destination other than you.

I have no idea where I will end up, not even sure what lies around the corner.

Fear: Can it ever be my friend?

I can't see and feel utterly burned out, yet you lead me.

In my blindness I cling to you, asking for strength for each day.

I entrust my children to you,

Aware that my failings as a parent may discourage and even scar them.

I simply trust that you will use me—imperfect—to make a difference in their lives.

May they grow up to be responsible, faithful and compassionate adults.

Forgive me for trying to make them into people they are not.

They are yours. I give them to you. No more control.

Trust grace.

Light of the world, lead me to you.

South Carolina home for six weeks.

CHAPTER 6

Wasting Time With Jesus

I HAVE DONE much reflective writing over the years but never regularly. A year ago, I began keeping a journal in anticipation of this renewal leave. I wanted to get into the habit of writing each day. Today, I read back over my journal and discover some common themes.

I refer to my upcoming leave with a mixture of excitement and anxiety:

Thanksgiving Day

I made a vow to do no church work today. After making Thanksgiving dinner, I spent the rest of the day folding wash, doing dishes, reading magazines and working with Talitha and Sarah on a game for the staff Christmas party. At one point, I began to wonder how I was going to make it through three months of no work. Will I go stir crazy? We'll see.

Mother's Day

As the rest of the family went to church tonight and I had the night off, I was wondering if I would feel lonely on my renewal leave. As I struggled with the choice of doing sermon work, reading a book or sitting by the lake, I asked myself: If I could do anything I wanted on my leave, would I rather be back home and busy? We'll see.

June

I was at a worship service tonight at our denominational annual conference. I felt pretty relaxed because I had no responsibilities and I was by myself. I was also dead tired by that time from being so harried. I began to imagine what it would be like to be on renewal leave and have absolutely nothing I had to do. I really could not fathom it, and I began to be a little anxious. I wondered, how will I really feel? Will I feel guilty, lonely, free, creative, depressed? I like to think I am going away so I can get reacquainted with myself—and with God.

August 8

I've been struggling with a respiratory infection. It was very good for me to hear my doctor encourage me about my renewal leave, saying that he had two months off about 10 years ago when switching practices. He said, "You'll have time to get to know yourself." I believe that as well, but sometimes when I say it to someone else, they look at me as if I'm crazy.

August 14

On Tuesday morning, I went to the dentist. While sitting in the chair, I began to think about my renewal leave and was just a little anxious. I am usually so very busy. I wondered how I would feel when it was all taken away from me immediately.

Funny thing is, I went to the hospital later in the morning to visit an elderly woman. She asked if I was ready for my leave. Without waiting for a reply, she said with a smile, "Well, I guess part of you is ready, and part of you isn't." She knew! She knew how difficult it is going to be for me.

August 16

One of my clergy colleagues says he needs a leave of absence because he is burned out and can no longer cope with parish ministry. He is not even sure he is suited for the parish. More and more, I see that I am not alone. Others, too, are becoming aware of an emptiness and weariness of spirit.

Another common theme in my journal is sleep deprivation. I go to bed too late and wake up too early, but my sleep is also often disrupted. My journal indicated a myriad of reasons:

- Gary was snoring at midnight, and I had to move to another bed.
- I had a hot flash at 12:30 a.m.
- Talitha's lamp fell on her head at 1 a.m., and she started crying.
- Our cat Shadrach was meowing outside our bedroom door at 1:30 a.m.
- Garth had the TV set on too loud at 2 a.m.
- Sarah turned on the microwave at 2:30 a.m.
- I had to go to the bathroom at 3 a.m.

- Sarah and a friend were talking outside my window at 3:30 a.m.
- Talitha had an excruciating earache at 4 a.m.
- Sarah woke up with pain in her chest at 4:30 a.m., and I had to call the emergency room.
- I heard beeping sounds in the kitchen at 5 a.m.—they came from the fan over the stove.
- Sarah called at 5:30 a.m. from a friend's house, saying she lost her car keys and wanted us to pick her up. I don't think so!
- The alarm went off at 6 a.m. Time to get up!

The most frequent theme in my journal is feeling continually exhausted from the hectic pace I set for myself. Here is a typical day:

- **6 a.m.:** Wake up, take a shower and get ready for the day.
- **6:30 a.m.:** Drive to the hospital to see a woman having surgery. I stay with her and her husband until she goes into surgery at 8 a.m.
- **8:15 a.m.:** I have to get gas but spill some on my suit. I rush home for 20 minutes, where I change my suit, check my email and send the job description for a staff opening to an interested person.
- **8:40 a.m.:** I take off for an all-day Board of Ordained Ministry meeting, for which I am the chairperson. I have to leave the meeting early, at 2:15 p.m., so I can get downtown for a 3 p.m. funeral at the church. Afterward, I follow through on some items from the earlier board meeting.
- **4:30 p.m.:** Gary and I visit a couple in their home about our campaign to raise money for the new building. By this time, I am really dragging. I did not exercise this morning, which is the only thing that really

keeps me going. I am feeling it now, but the day is not over.

- **6 p.m.:** I drive to Grandville to meet a family at the funeral home to talk about another funeral on Saturday, staying for an hour.
- **7:50 p.m.:** I arrive back home, eat some salad and a piece of pizza, then take Talitha with me back to the hospital to see how the woman came through surgery. On the way home, we stop at the drugstore.
- **8:45 p.m.:** I change and try to read the paper but cannot keep my eyes open.
- **9:30 p.m.:** I go to bed, but as I am drifting off to sleep, we get a call from Sarah. Gary mercifully goes downstairs to talk with her so I can sleep.

In the midst of the busyness and chaos that characterize my life, sometimes things turn really bizarre—like an incident on December 14, 2000. I woke up at 5:15 a.m. to go to my exercise class. When I went to get into my car, I noticed it wasn't there. I looked up and down the street and it wasn't there, either. I then went upstairs to rouse Sarah, who was sound asleep.

"Sarah, where's my car? I need my car. Where's my car?"

"It's in a ditch."

"It's where?"

"The car slid off the road into a snow bank."

"Where is it?"

"Somewhere along 28th Street, I think."

"Is it off the road or blocking a lane?"

"I think it's partly in the road."

"How did you get home?"

"A guy took me home."

"Who was he?"

"I don't know. He just stopped, and I asked him for a ride."

"Why didn't you tell us when you got home?"

"I didn't want to wake you up."

"Well, you woke us up now."

At that point, I knew my exercise class was not to be. I reluctantly woke Gary, we made Sarah get up and the three of us got in the van. We found two shovels and tried to dress warmly because it was frigid. Upon further questioning, Sarah said the car was near the Farmer's Market on Fulton Street, so off we went. Sure enough, the car was on Fulton in a snow bank across from Salvation Army.

The car was really wedged in tight, so it took a good half hour of shoveling to get enough snow away that Gary could rock it out. We tried to patiently explain to Sarah why she should have called us right away or awakened us and why it was really stupid to leave the car—especially when it was blocking a lane on one of the busiest streets in Grand Rapids!

As I pondered my journal from last year, these were my thoughts: *I can't believe I kept up that kind of pace. It's insane. I can't and don't want to live that way anymore. I still want to be an effective pastor. Nothing will change unless I am willing to put God first. God needs to come before church.*

* * *

During my renewal leave, I have chosen to enter the desert. No, I am not living in a literal desert. Far from it! I am living very comfortably in South Carolina. As David Rensberger puts it, the Greek word which is usually a translation of "desert" or "wilderness" is *eremos*, which means "deserted" or "solitary." *Eremos* is a place where there are no people.

From *eremos* we get the word eremite, which is a person who lives in a deserted space; in other words, a hermit. We usually think of a hermit as someone who goes off to live alone, at times as part of a religious quest. From the early centuries of Christianity, hermits have gone to the Egyptian and Syrian deserts. Why? In order to find God. That's it. In order to find God.

Sometimes the only way to find God is to let go of all the distractions that hinder our quest. That's exactly what I am doing. I have gone to the *eremos* to live the solitary life of an eremite in order to find God and myself. Thomas Merton has written that when we are really alone we are with God.

I now have a much better sense of the internal struggles Jesus encountered at the beginning of his ministry during his 40 days in the desert. Without other people or responsibilities to deter me, I am left alone with God and myself, which has been rather terrifying at times. By entering into the painful process of self-revelation by being totally honest about who I am and stripping away layer upon layer of pretense, I have been completely exposed before God. I have acknowledged all the things and people I love more than God. Only after this happens can God begin to remake me into the person God intends me to be.

A friend emailed me the other day, "Have you gotten to know anyone?" I replied, "Are you kidding? That's the last thing I want to do. I have two goals in this time away: to know myself and to know God. That's it. I am in solitude."

I know that the desert will not be the end for me. I have been called to go through the desert so that I can minister in all the deserts around me in Grand Rapids. Just as Peter suggested staying on the mountaintop with Moses, Elijah and Jesus during his transfiguration, so is it tempting to stay right here, just God and me. I do not believe that is what God intends for me, however. Transformed and remolded into God's image, I will go back into my world with renewed energy, commitment and love for God and others.

* * *

I reach a catharsis today. This morning, in my devotions, I read the story of Mary and Martha (Luke 10:38-42). I know this passage very well. In fact, it was the text of the first "real" sermon I ever preached 20 years ago to my first congregation. This story also has a special place in my heart because my beloved grandmothers were named Mary and Martha. They actually seemed to fit the personalities of these two special friends of Jesus.

Like most people, I have always contrasted the two sisters: Martha, characterized by action, service and doing; and Mary, by contemplation, prayer and being. I have always been more like Martha than Mary. I am a doer. I am task-oriented. I won't sit down until everything on the list is completed. For years, I have reluctantly viewed this Scripture as making prayer more important than service. Naturally, that heaps on the guilt since I find it very difficult to simply be. Sitting in one spot praying for half an hour is almost like torture!

This morning it suddenly dawns on me. When Jesus said to Martha, "Mary has chosen the better part," he was not chiding Martha for being a busybody. Nor was he calling her to task for taking care of his needs. No, it was Martha's worry and distraction that concerned Jesus. The obstacle in Martha's path was not her commitment to service, it was her attitude. She was not wholly present to Jesus as Mary was because she allowed her hostess role to get in the way. The one thing needed was to be present to Jesus.

As I contemplate my own life, I realize that this has been precisely my struggle. I will always be a doer. I will always attend to details. I will always be committed to service. But as long as I allow the tasks of ministry to overwhelm me, I will be distracted and worried and will miss what is truly needed: to be present to God.

As long as I pay attention to the voices of everyone else and ignore God's voice, I will not be open to the voice of the Spirit within and all around me. Until I learn how to let go of many things, I will not be able to go deeper—to move beyond my constant anxiety and rest in the heart of Jesus. Until I take time to sit and listen at Jesus' feet, I will not hear God's gentle voice.

This afternoon, as I am driving home from a few errands, I listen to selections from *Phantom of the Opera*. Suddenly, as often happens with music, the words begin speaking to me and I start to sob—not cry, sob. I even have to pull off the road for a while. In the songs, "Music of the Night" and "All I Ask of You," I hear God gently singing to me: "I'm here to guide you and calm you and set you free. You are safe with me. Your fears are far behind you because I walk beside you. Let me go with you. I have great plans for you. I am going to use you in a mighty way. Just remember, there is need of only one thing. All I ask is that you love me. That's all I ask—love me."

The light of God's love surrounds me in the car. Then it begins to rain. They are God's tears of joy. Perhaps I am finally getting it. It only rains for a minute—not a drop of rain the rest of the day. It is a mystical experience I will never be able to adequately explain. All I know is that I became aware of God's radical love for me and for the world and it transformed me.

* * *

As I become truly present to and love God at all times, I am learning to pay attention to everything going on around me. Every day, I spend time outdoors running, walking or biking, and my prayer before I leave is always that I see God in everything I encounter. Indeed, symbols of the divine are everywhere. All nature communicates faith by pointing beyond itself to God.

- According to tradition, in times of famine the pelican tears open its breast to feed its young with its lifeblood. It's a symbol of salvation through the blood of Jesus Christ.
- The freedom of the seagull reminds me of our freedom to respond to Christ in faith and invite Jesus to walk with us.
- After losing an arm, the starfish is able to regenerate and grow a new arm. So God can bring healing and hope into the darkest corners of our lives.

- The deer reminds me of my yearning for God, "As a deer longs for life-giving water, so my soul longs for you, O God." (Psalm 42:1)
- The fish has been an ancient symbol for Jesus Christ since the earliest of years of Christianity.
- The ebb and flow of the tides reminds me of the constancy of God's love in sending Jesus Christ, who is the same yesterday, today and tomorrow.
- The rainbow is a sign of God's everlasting covenant with human beings and with every living creature on earth.
- The tall and straight sea pines are like my soul, which reaches heavenward toward God.
- If God has the stars in the heaven and the sand on the beach and the birds of the air numbered, then surely God cares for me.
- The alligator, jellyfish and snake reinforce my determination to keep a distance from those things that would separate me from God.
- The graceful path of the dolphin reminds me of the beauty of lives that reveal the grace of God through Jesus Christ.
- The omnipresent vines are a symbol of how Jesus said he is the vine and we are the branches, who can only bear fruit when we abide in the vine. (John 15:5)
- The seashell is an ancient symbol for baptism, a reminder that at my baptism God said to me the same words God said to Jesus, "You are my Daughter, the Beloved; with you I am well pleased." (Mark 1:11)

* * *

Last night, 15-year-old Talitha went to the Homecoming Dance at a neighboring high school. She was invited by someone she met through church camp. I regret not being a part of the excitement of buying a dress, shoes and purse and getting hair and nails done, yet I was glad that Gary's parents were visiting and could run her around.

Of our three children, Talitha is the most like me. She is intense, focused, highly intelligent, studies hard and is organized in her life and thinking. She has a good head on her shoulders and is a high achiever. Unlike me, she has such a wide circle of friends that I can't possibly keep track of them all. She knows how to have fun and doesn't sit home on the weekends studying. She also loves to shop, which is the bane of my existence. As a little girl, Talitha used to change outfits five or six times a day. Now that she is older, I can drop her and her friends off at the mall where they spend hours. When I do accompany her, I take a book along and read in the dressing room while she tries on clothes to her heart's content.

My favorite story of Talitha happened when she was 2 and a half years old. One cold morning in November, I was out jogging and Gary was working at the computer. Talitha quietly unlocked the front door and escaped. In a panic, Gary jumped in the car and combed the streets but could not find her. When he got home, the phone rang. Evidently, Talitha had run a third of a mile to the school to visit Garth in kindergarten. Unfortunately, she was not wearing a coat—or shoes! It's a wonder we weren't cited for child neglect.

Talitha is well adjusted and knows who she is. She has discovered running and has been successful on the high school cross-country team. Talitha is a very articulate teenager and a force to be reckoned with when she is upset. She has the potential to do anything she wants in life, and I will be eager to see in what direction she will head.

* * *

A common theme in my recent spiritual struggle has been allowing the Spirit to master me. Learning to grow in my spiritual life is not something I can do. It is something I allow to happen to me. Letting go reminds me of God's prevenient grace. I cannot open my life to God unless God's love is prompting me. The apostle Paul writes in Galatians 2:20 that when we are justified by God's grace, it is no longer we who live, but Christ who lives in us.

What I want more than anything is for Christ to live in me and through me, fully and completely. In my devotions this morning, I see a familiar passage in an entirely new way. I am reading John 15:1-5 where Jesus says that he is the true vine and that just as a branch cannot bear fruit by itself unless it abides in the vine, neither can we bear fruit unless we abide in him.

In the Old Testament, the grapevine was a symbol for Israel. In Isaiah 5:1-10, however, we read that Israel had only produced wild grapes, not the kind of fruit for which God had hoped. In the gospel of John, the vine is used in an entirely new way. Now, Jesus becomes the vine. Jesus has taken Israel's place. Jesus, the vine, has become the lifeline to God and we humans are the branches.

We are called to bear fruit but can only produce that fruit when we remain connected to the vine. Branches can't live apart from the vine. When we allow the vine to produce fruit through us and give up our will and our lives for the vine, then we live in communion with God. We quietly allow Jesus to produce fruit in us rather than think we have to do more and more for God.

It's an odd concept for a doer like me. In John 15:5, Jesus says that apart from him we can do nothing. I don't know if I have it in me to wait around for God. I can't just sit around when things are falling apart. I have such an inner drive to accomplish that there has been little room to receive God's power. But that's our call—not to barrel on ahead but to move ourselves out of the way so God can get to work in us. It's going to take a little reimagining, a lot of faith and even an act of will for me to let go that much. But that's what the word "abide" means. We are called to rest in Jesus, relax and let Jesus hold us, and allow God's energy to flow through us. We offer our very lives so that Jesus can produce fruit in us.

But there's more. Jesus says that we are to abide in his love just as he abides in God's love. And how do we abide in his love? By loving one another as Jesus has loved us. There is no greater love than to lay down one's life for one's friends (John 15:12). The fruit we bear is nothing more than the love of Jesus, which we allow to shine through us. That's the key.

Remaining connected to the vine of Jesus Christ is a continual process of letting the Spirit flow in us by loving God, self and others. It is no longer we who live, but it is Christ who lives in us (Galatians 2:20).

As I ponder my role as a branch on the vine of Jesus Christ, I begin thinking about my colleagues on the staff of First United Methodist Church. In a way, Gary, our staff and I are all shoots on the thick branch of First Church, which is grafted onto the vine of Jesus Christ. Each staff member has responsibility for a particular area of the corporate life of First Church but with a common goal as expressed in our mission statement. Although the mission statement is in the process of being revised, it is still a fairly accurate representation of who we are as a body of Christ.

"It is the mission of First United Methodist Church to call people into relationship with Christ, to experience God's love and to make all of our actions a response to that love. Our mission is shaped by the Wesleyan emphases of a vital personal faith, social justice, ecumenism and a global concern. We will accomplish this mission by:

- Being a large and friendly downtown church, drawing members from all areas of metropolitan Grand Rapids.
- Embracing all people as sisters and brothers.
- Engaging in a broad range of ministries.
- Offering inspiring worship.
- Providing challenging educational experiences.

- Involving people in service.
- Nurturing one another."

When our beloved administrative assistant retired last year after 36 years on staff, I asked her, "What advice do you have for me? How can I be a better pastor?" She said, "Love your staff. Spend time with your staff. Let them know how much you appreciate them." I believe we have the best church staff in the world. Every person on our staff is a committed disciple of Jesus Christ and dedicated to fulfilling the mission of First Church. They are specialists in their area, yet they are also aware of the need to work together to accomplish goals.

This past summer we decided that we needed a staff covenant: a written document that facilitates our life and work together. When I come back from my renewal leave, we'll put it together, but I've already done a lot of thinking about the importance of our staff. I've determined that every time we hire a new staff member, I want to share with him or her these suggestions:

- Take care of yourself, spiritually, emotionally and physically. Work hard. Give us your best, but take time for yourself or you will burn out.
- A primary aspect of your job is to empower others for ministry. Your role is to identify, equip, train and supervise others for ministry.
- We are all team players at First Church. No area of ministry is more important than any other area. We are not competing against each other but are in ministry with each other. We all have a common goal and so must support each other.
- You must show loyalty to other staff. Never criticize a staff member in public or to another staff member. If you have a concern, go directly to that person and talk it out.

- Confidentiality is critical. What is said at staff meetings stays within the group unless permission is given to share the information.
- Strive for excellence at all times. You can do far more than you think you can. Do not be afraid to risk or fail. Remember Philippians 4:13, "I can do all things through him who strengthens me."
- Take care of one another on the staff. We are a family within the family of the church. Support staff members by attending events they sponsor, even if you don't have to be there.
- Remember that you are a shoot connected to the branch of First Church, which is connected to the vine of Jesus Christ. You are not the vine yourself. Allow God's love to bear fruit in you.

I am indebted to the staff at First Church for all they have taught me in the last eight years. I am in awe of their skills, their spiritual depth and their support. It is a true joy to be a pastor at First Church!

* * *

Two days ago, President Bush gave the go ahead to bomb terrorist targets in Afghanistan in an effort to undercut the Taliban militia sheltering Osama bin Laden and bolster opposition forces fighting the Taliban. I have been in the unique position of having been away from home the entire time—except for two days—since September 11. Because I am living pretty much in solitude, I have not had the opportunity to discuss current events with my congregation or with others.

However, through reading the paper, watching the news and observing what is going around me, I sense a unity in our country that I've never experienced in my lifetime. In my travels across the country since the attacks, I have seen countless cars with flags, homes with patriotic symbols displayed and people wearing flag pins or patriotic shirts as an expression of solidarity with those whose lives were lost. Tens of millions of dollars have been raised. Our country is very different than it was just five weeks ago. I sense that people are kinder and more compassionate with each other. My prayer is that this tragedy will serve as an opportunity for all of us to take a close look at the pervasiveness of violence in our own cities, states and homes and renew our commitment to love and value all people.

I grew up during the Vietnam War and, as a Mennonite, was part of one of the historic peace churches. I went with a busload of church people to an anti-war demonstration in Washington, D.C., in 1969. The divisions our country experienced during the Vietnam era were terribly painful, even for teenagers like me.

I am sensing little of that opposition now, primarily because we were the victims. The terrorist attacks on the World Trade Center and the Pentagon were so horrifying and the loss of life so staggering that we have all needed to rally around each other for comfort, hope and strength. We have also looked to our leaders for calmness and wisdom.

I have mixed emotions about our assault on Afghanistan. Having grown up in a peace church, I believe that force should only be a last resort and should in no instance be directed toward innocent civilians. Attacking an entire country because of a small group of terrorists seems unacceptable to me. My hope is that we could capture Osama bin Laden and let the world bring him to justice. However, I also appreciate how difficult and delicate that task is.

I trust that President Bush has surrounded himself with good advisers and is undergirding his decisions with faith. Religion is a part of President Bush's daily life, not a gimmick used to court the public's favor. He has said that his faith enabled him to deal with an alcohol problem and helped him find a vocation in politics. According to a recent article in *USA Today*, President Bush told a news network that he finds great comfort in his faith. It helps him remember that although he has a lot of responsibility, he is just a person—a simple human being seeking redemption, solace and strength through something greater than himself.

I have a vivid memory of the day President Bush was inaugurated. For some reason, I was watching the celebration on television and I distinctly remember the eyes. As George W. Bush walked through the crowds to be inaugurated, his eyes looked so focused. It was if he were looking right through everyone and everything to God, who was giving him the strength to take on the incredible responsibility of being president. The intensity of his eyes conveyed not only resolve but also humility and a dependence on God. I pray for President Bush and his advisers every day, trusting that faith will permeate all their decisions.

* * *

I hadn't thought about this story for years. Garth and Talitha were in the middle of a fight. Tears and angry words flew about the room. Normally, I let the children resolve their own differences, but this dispute called for parental action.

"What's wrong?" I asked.

"Garth won't let me play his harmonica!" Talitha sobbed. I never knew Garth had a harmonica, so I called him into the room.

"What's this about a harmonica, Garth?"

"Mom, I found a harmonica out on the street this afternoon, and I don't want Talitha to play it."

"Why not?"

"Because I'm collecting harmonicas."

"Oh, really? Since when?"

"Since yesterday. Now I have two harmonicas, and because I'm collecting them, nobody else can touch them."

I didn't buy his story and told Garth that if he was not going to play the harmonica himself, he had to share and let Talitha use it. Garth absolutely refused. He stormed into his room, shut the door and proceeded to sulk. Fifteen minutes later he came into my room and said, "Mom, I just threw the harmonica out the window. I decided it was causing me too much trouble."

It was an incredible insight for a 10-year-old boy. Garth realized that the harmonica wasn't worth holding on to. It wasn't worth the conflict it was causing. Garth didn't have any interest in harmonicas anyway. He was simply using it as a way to provoke his younger sister. When it dawned on Garth that he was not going to get his way, he wisely gave up. He didn't need to get into trouble over a dirty, bent harmonica.

I can think of a whole lot of harmonicas I need to throw out the window. Having the opportunity to step back from active ministry for a few months, I am beginning to realize the unnecessary baggage I carry with me. To live a whole, spiritually healthy life centered in God, I need to throw away some stuff:

- The feeling that I am indispensable.
- The craving for recognition.
- The desire for attention.
- The need to be right.
- Anger when I don't get my way.
- Bitterness toward people who have hurt me.
- The inability to call it quits and relax.
- An obsession with work.
- The insistence that I don't have time to nurture my spirit.

Of course, I can think of countless harmonicas others throw out the window as well, but I've decided to focus on myself. As we all know, the only person we can change is ourselves. I'm going to start and end with me.

* * *

I feel like such an idiot. I have a difficult extended family conversation tonight on the phone and I blow it. I do not handle the call in the right away. When it's over, I storm around the condo, calling myself all the bad words I know, which, admittedly, are not many. I can't believe I made the situation worse than it was before. I even asked God to help me say the right words. It didn't work.

Conflict resolution is something I do often at church. When people spend a lot of time around each other, there are bound to be occasional tensions. I am grateful that we do not have major conflicts among our staff, but we do have our moments, especially when it's a busy time in the church year and we're all feeling stressed. There are also times when church members become angry with one another—or with me.

The best method for solving a problem is for the conflicted parties to sit down together and simply talk it out. Sometimes that is best done with a mediator. What's most important is for both parties to want to solve the conflict. Another key is a willingness to take the high road. I think I have used that phrase more than any other when counseling with people in conflict. When tempted to seek revenge, become bitter or lash out in anger, I encourage people to always take the high road. When others have hurt you, don't return evil for evil. Love your enemies and pray for those who persecute you. Sound familiar? Remember the Golden Rule: "In everything do to others as you would have them do to you" (Matthew 7:12). It's too bad I didn't practice what I preach in my phone conversation tonight.

After fussing and stewing, I finally go outside. I walk around for a little while and check the mailbox, which I forgot to do earlier in the day. Wouldn't you know it? I receive the most wonderfully affirming note from someone in the church for whom I care a great deal. It is exactly what I need at that moment, to know that even when I do the stupidest things, there is still grace.

This letter is a keeper. Even though I am known for throwing away items at the drop of a hat, I do keep letters. I keep them all! Naturally, not all of the letters I receive are positive or encouraging. It goes with the territory of being a pastor. And I don't always react well to nasty letters. It usually takes 20 positive letters to take the sting out of one mean-spirited letter.

But I thank God that most of the cards I receive are positive. Isn't it incredible how a card or letter can make your day? It takes such little effort—taking a few minutes to dash off a note to someone you appreciate. But the effects can last a lifetime. Some of the most encouraging notes I keep in my Day-Timer and briefcase. When I'm having a bad day, I often read a note to bolster my spirits. Encouraging notes remind me that, despite my failures, shortcomings and struggles, there are still those who love me. And if others love me, how much more does God love and care for me?

I'm not sure what I am going to do about the phone call tonight. I suspect I will write an encouraging note, throw out a harmonica or two—and take the high road.

* * *

When I awake in the morning, it is always dark. I open the blinds and crawl back into bed for my devotional time. I keep my eye on the sliding glass door, though, looking for that first ray of sunlight to touch the top of the trees. Sometimes I can see the early morning moon from my bedroom, but I can always hear the birds. Lying in bed, I watch the trees, checking to see which birds will appear by the window. I can usually count on a pair of blue jays to grace this quiet time with God.

After an hour or so, I wander downstairs, open all the curtains and have my worship time. I light a candle, which is surrounded by an assortment of shells, starfish and pine cones, symbols of God's creation. Then I sing, read Scripture and pray. It's a great way to start the day.

Then it's time for my run. I began to run regularly in July 1979, one year after Gary and I were married. I had been active in team sports all my life: field hockey, basketball, softball and volleyball, but once I was out of school, I had to search for other ways to keep fit. Actually, Gary got me running sporadically in seminary. Running seemed a perfect sport because I didn't need a partner (an introvert's dream) and I could run when and where I wanted by just going out the door. It satisfied my desire to be outside.

I started out humbly, running around the block. By Labor Day I was up to three miles and stayed there until after Christmas, when I progressed to four, then five miles. I still remember the exhilaration and soreness I felt the first time I ran five miles on the indoor track at Payne-Whitney gymnasium at Yale University.

In May 1980, I ran in my first 10-kilometer race in Milford, Connecticut, where we lived, and I haven't looked back since. It is difficult to overestimate the significance that running has had on my life. Running has become part of who I am. I usually take one day off a week from running. If I take any more days off, people know I've got to be deathly sick. I've run all over the world, at all times of the day and night, and in all kinds of conditions: pouring rain, 100-degree heat, sub-zero temperatures, blizzards and pure ice.

As I gained more experience in running, I decided to tackle longer races and eventually ran two marathons (26.2 miles) in 1984. I also ventured into triathlons and completed my first triathlon (swimming, biking, running) in the summer of 1985. I was in the early stages of pregnancy with Talitha but insisted on doing the race, which was probably not a good idea because I felt so sick.

As my children grew, I ran less and spent more time coaching their sports teams and watching their games. I was also in full-time ministry and didn't have time to train seriously. It wasn't until five years ago that I got back into long distance running. Because of family difficulties, I resorted to the best way I knew how to relieve stress. Go out for a nice, long run. This time, my goal was not only to run a marathon again but to participate in the Boston Marathon, the only road race in the world for which you have to qualify.

By running well at the Chicago Marathon four years ago, I qualified for Boston and have run the Boston Marathon the last three years. I am already registered for next year's run. Training for the Boston Marathon every winter has been a joy. I love challenges of all kinds but especially those that stretch this old body to the limit. This is why I keep getting up early every morning to run, whether I feel like it or not.

When I run, I am free. Whatever burdens I am carrying are put aside for an hour, and I become one with my body and with God. I guess you might say it's the one recess I allow myself every day. Running is what keeps me sane. It's the only time of day when I am completely alone: no phone calls, no interruptions, no emergencies. It's a time either to completely clear my mind or think through difficult issues.

I have occasionally characterized my running as "wasting time with Jesus." Marathon training plans often warn against empty miles. If you are serious about a race, you can't just go out and run. To train effectively, you have to get your heart rate up by doing hill repeats, intervals on the track and occasionally running at your race pace or faster. I know that, but I still like empty miles because there are no other empty moments in my life. I enjoy wasting time with Jesus. On these long, lazy runs, my mind is free to pray, wander and enjoy God's presence in this beautiful world.

I am not done with challenging my body. This past summer I participated in a half-ironman triathlon: 1.2 miles swimming, 56 miles biking and 13.1 miles running, and I loved every minute of it. Now I'm thinking really long: a 50-mile running race or a full ironman triathlon (2.4 miles swimming, 112 miles biking, 26.2 miles running). Yes, I am crazy, but I just might do it someday!

* * *

Today is the one-month anniversary of the terrorist attacks on September 11. In an ironic twist, which I did not know at the time, September 11 was also International Day of Peace.

The Peace Bell at the United Nations was to be rung to initiate the opening session of the General Assembly.

The Desert

I can't pretend anymore, God.

I have to leave, enter the wilderness of my own pain.

Like the hermits of old, I exit the life I know to be with God in the eremos.

I am exposed, naked, bereft of all security.

So this is what cold turkey feels like.

A barren place to be, yet my senses are on high alert.

I see hear smell taste touch your holiness everywhere. I am not alone.

I want to be wholly present to you, to rest in the heart of Jesus.

The beauty is indescribable; my desert spirit is home.

Rest in the heart of Jesus;

Abide in him; don't plow on ahead;

Wasting time with Jesus.

I am fully alive.

Best place to waste time with Jesus.

CHAPTER 7

Playing

TODAY I BOOK flights to France for Gary and me. I have rescheduled my pilgrimage to the monastic community of Taizé for the first full week of November. Gary will then join me in Paris the second week of November. I am thrilled that he is able to rearrange his schedule to take that time off. This fall has been very difficult for Gary with me gone. When we are both at the church, we each work 60 to 70 hours a week. So, I can imagine how chaotic it must be for him right now. It's nice that Gary's mother and father are visiting from Florida for a few weeks to help out.

Gary and I are often asked, "What is it like to be a clergy couple? And what is it like to be co-pastors in the same church?" Before coming to Grand Rapids, we always worked in separate churches. We decided we would make a good team, however, and requested of our bishop and cabinet that they try to find a place where we could serve together.

The reasons to share one ministry were compelling:

- Our skills complement each other. While we are very different in the way we work and in many of the gifts we bring, we share the same vision for ministry.
- We discovered that parenting three children while serving two different churches was a challenge. While our children enjoyed having friends in two churches, there was always a subtle tension. Which church were they going to this week, Mommy's church or Daddy's church? In whose Christmas pageant would they participate? In whose choir would they sing? Our family was never together on Sundays. More than that, as PKs (preachers' kids), our children knew our attention was focused elsewhere on Sunday, so they often chose that time to act out. We learned to expect it, laugh at it and go with the flow.
- Constant night meetings and emergencies created child care headaches and a nagging sense of guilt for being absentee parents. Serving in the same church, there was a better chance for one of us to be home most evenings.
- We wanted to model a sense of pastoral colleagueship and male/female equality. We decided that to work together we would receive exactly the same salary and divide pastoral responsibilities in a way that demonstrated both equality and the best use of our gifts.

After eight years of working together, I think we would both say co-pastoring is all that we had hoped it to be. Our children have a sense of stability by being rooted in one church. We have the freedom to decide who will respond to an emergency. When our children are participating in school activities, one of us can usually be there. Most of all, our congregation has given us unqualified support. Our family has gone through some rocky times in the last five years and I know we wouldn't have made it if it hadn't been for the love, care and prayers of our congregation.

Our professional relationship also continues to evolve. Communication is critical. Gary and I are constantly negotiating responsibilities, clarifying calendars and filling each other in on pastoral needs. We also are growing in our acceptance of each other. Working with one's spouse calls for the exercise of the best fruit the Christian spirit can produce: particularly peace, patience, kindness, gentleness and self-control. We recognize that we are very different people in nature, temperament, procedure and instinct. The opposing traits that attract one person to the other can also be the most trying ones when cooperating in constant, close and rarely ending work. We do keep trying to move one another to "Christian perfection" by cultivating patience and good humor.

Because we work in close proximity in every phase of our life—work, marriage, and parenting—we have discovered the necessity of creating space to pursue personal interests and friendships. Even though we are co-pastors, we still are individuals. We acknowledge our inability to fulfill each other's every need. Our individual wholeness as well as the health of our marriage depends upon cultivating our spiritual lives and widening the circle of our friendship and support.

Hence, I am taking a renewal leave by myself. I need this time to tend to my spirit as well as pursue my own interests and desires. When Gary takes his renewal leave, I am sure he will do something entirely different. That's as it should be. I'm sure glad he will be joining me in Paris, though. We're going to have a great time!

* * *

I attend a wonderful worship service this morning. The music is outstanding, the flow of the service is smooth and easy, the pastors seem comfortable with their roles and the sermon is very good. I suspect the primary reason I like the service is because it closely approximates worship at First Church!

I never fail to be moved by excellence. Whether it is listening to a musical performer, watching a play, observing a teacher at work, pondering a work of art, reading a fine novel or hearing an outstanding sermon, I appreciate excellence—especially because I know how much time and effort it takes to cultivate excellence. I have always told my children that it is important to do their best in everything they attempt. I remind them that they will not be good at everything they do. But, if they work hard and try their very best with the gifts and skills they have, God is pleased and that's all that matters. I also emphasize that every person in this world is excellent at something and part of the joy of human life is finding out what that is.

What I appreciate most this morning is the excellent organ music. The organist plays difficult music with confidence, energy and skill. I am not sure I could ever be a pastor in a church that doesn't use an organ regularly. Praise bands alone just don't do it for me. Having studied the organ for many years, I find that organ music beckons me beyond the present into the mysterious presence of the holy in a way that other instrumental music does not.

In 1979, on my 25th birthday, I gave an organ recital at my home church in Pennsylvania. The next day I wrote about what it felt like to prepare and perform the recital. Reading it 22 years later, I was astonished that my reflections could apply to preaching sermons as well as to almost any other significant human endeavor. This is part of what I penned:

> *All people have peak experiences in their lives, moments that have made such an impression on them that they will never be forgotten, moments that in some way or another affect the rest of their lives. Such was my experience during last night's organ recital.*

For someone who is not a musician, it is difficult to express in words how one goes about learning a piece of music, for the acquiring of technical mastery is only the first step. One must somehow get inside the music itself and learn to make the music come alive. When one spends so many hours for a single recital of all new music, a certain rapport develops between the musician and the music. The job is to make the music one's own. If one has nothing to give, there is no sense in performing, for the music will be lifeless, and there will be no meaning to it.

For me, to play the organ is to praise God for all that God has given me, especially for whatever small musical talents I may have. Therefore, when I play an organ recital, my goal is the communication of Christian truths through the medium of music, which is one of the most pervasive and subtle yet most wonderful means of glorifying God.

When I am playing, I try to concentrate on making music, not hitting every note right. The most important thing is to communicate my love of music and my love of God and to express the intense connection that has developed between the music and me during those many hours of practice.

Today, I do not play the organ much anymore, but my theology of organ playing is a theology of life and carries through into everything I do. This past May, when we recognized our graduating high school seniors in worship, I shared with them my recent musings about what makes for a healthy, satisfying and joy-filled life:

- Don't underestimate yourself. You have far more to give to this world than you might imagine. The untapped potential inside of you is amazing.

- Don't underestimate God. I truly believe that it is faith in God that gives us the strength and energy to deal with whatever life throws at us.
- Don't be afraid to risk. One of my favorite quotes comes from T.S. Eliott: "Only those who will risk going too far can possibly find out how far one can go."
- Don't give up. One of the noblest qualities we can have is perseverance. Nothing worthwhile comes easily. When you get discouraged, remember, "This, too, shall pass." When things don't go well, remember, there will be another day. When you feel like quitting, remember that we all have within us that extra bit of determination to make it to the end.
- Dream big. The whole world is open to you. You can be or do anything you want. The future of our world lies with you. Go for it!
- Discover your gifts. I believe that everyone has God-given talents, skills at which we are good. But we also have spiritual gifts, which are special and unique gifts given to us by God in order to make a difference in the world. Cultivate your talents, but don't forget your spiritual gifts.
- Surround yourself with people who encourage and build you up. Your friends and family are your greatest supporters. Accept their love and help.
- Be in touch with your spirit. Don't be so busy that you forget to cultivate your inner life. Get to know yourself. Be self-aware. When in doubt, follow your heart.
- Remember what is important in life. I don't recall anyone getting to the end of life and asking for his or her sports car, sailboat or summer house. No, they ask for the presence of their loved ones. Don't let things become more important than people.

- Remember these words of Jesus from Luke 12:48, "From everyone to whom much has been given, much will be required." You have all been given wonderful gifts and opportunities. Don't forget that life gains meaning when we turn outward and give our lives in service to others.
- Finally, remember that God loves you no matter what. I trust that the days ahead will be exciting, challenging and fulfilling. I know there will be many good times. But there will also be times when you feel disappointment, failure or despair. Never forget that no matter what happens, God will always love you.

I said they were musings, but it's really my theology. It's what I know and believe about God. It's about allowing God to be glorified in us whatever we do in life. It's about becoming all that God wants us to be and all that we are capable of becoming. It's about communicating the love of God in everything we do. It's about excellence. The apostle Paul says in Philippians 4:8 that if there is any excellence or anything worthy of praise, we ought to think about whatever is true, whatever is honorable, whatever is just, whatever is pure, whatever is pleasing, and whatever is commendable.

* * *

My renewal leave is half over. I have been gone six weeks. My time away so far has been more than I could have hoped for. I believe that my *capax Dei*, my capacity for God, has grown and matured by tending to my inner life.

God has appeared to me in so many ways in the last six weeks: in plants and trees, in birds and animals, in water and sand, in sun and sky, in people and events, in tragedy and compassionate caring, in songs and hymns, in preaching and communion, in Scripture and novels, in prayer and meditation.

I never expected God to appear in a blaze of glory. After all, no one has ever seen God. When Moses had received the tablets of the law on the top of Mount Sinai, it was taking longer than the Israelites expected. They began to grumble, saying to Moses' brother, who was in charge, "Come on, Aaron, we don't know where Moses is or whether he is even coming back. Let's make some gods ourselves out of gold." Moses was so mad when he came down the mountain that he broke the tablets of the law, burned the golden calf, ground it to powder, scattered it on the water and made the Israelites drink it (Exodus 32).

After cooling down, Moses successfully interceded for his people to God. He pleaded for God to continue walking with the Israelites and said, "Show me your glory, I pray." God answered, "You are not going to see my face; for no one shall see me and live." God then told Moses to stand in a cleft in a rock. God would put a hand over Moses' eyes while God passed by, then release the hand so Moses would see God's backside! "But my face shall not be seen" (Exodus 33:17-23).

The backside of God is all we humans can see, but it's all we need. A frontal view of God in infinite glory, might, power and light would be more than we could take. So we are left with small images here and there of a God who longs to be seen: God in small doses. I am discovering that the signs are everywhere. They are vivid and specific yet at the same time mysterious and hidden. How could I have missed them for so long? I just haven't been paying attention.

I've decided that God's particular sign for me is the butterfly. Butterflies follow me everywhere: running, biking, driving, on the golf course and sitting at the beach. They don't bother me at all. They are just there, beckoning me to see God's backside.

What is happening now is the easy part, however. The temptation is always to stay on the mountain. But the journey of the spirit is not about removing oneself from the world. It's about finding sustenance and meaning in the very midst of everyday life. Having encountered the holy in so many ways, I realize that nurturing my spirit will be a far more complex endeavor when I get home. I am prepared for discomfort and perhaps even conflict as I re-enter a world that is carrying on quite nicely without me.

The changes in my inner life are going to demand some outward changes, and that means readjustment and reorientation, not only for me but also for my family and church. Most of all, it will mean more letting go of ambition, pride, attention and achievement. It will mean a continual emptying of myself and allowing the Spirit to master me

I have even had the fleeting thought that perhaps I should leave pastoral ministry, that it's going to be too difficult to return to the chaos and never-ending demands. Fortunately, I let that idea fly away quickly, for I still feel called to ministry in the local church. There is nothing else I want to do. I believe my spiritual gifts and talents are best suited to being a pastor. But I'm a little anxious about getting caught up again in a pace I don't believe I can sustain any longer. If only I can learn to abide in God's love and leave myself behind, with all my plans and projects and tasks. "Love me," God says. "Simply love me."

Light of the world, lead me to you.

* * *

Today I stop by one of the churches I had visited to pick up a cassette copy of the sermon. The pastor had preached a fine sermon on marriage, and I wanted to use some of the material for weddings. Without a doubt, the most challenging task I have as a pastor is preaching. When my children moan and groan about a six-page paper, I remind them that Dad and I have to write the equivalent of a 12-page paper every other week! And that's just one small part of what we do.

I have always worked on my sermons far in advance of when I preach them. They are not ready to preach till Sunday morning, but I tweak them for weeks. Gary and I try to plan our sermon schedule at least six months ahead of time, and we normally alternate preaching every other Sunday. In a large church where music, the arts and education all play a coordinated role in worship, everyone needs adequate time to plan and prepare.

I make a file on my computer for each Sunday I am preaching. I read the Scriptures over and over so I'm familiar with the themes. I also bring home from the church all the commentaries and books in my library that have anything to do with the theme. Then I let my subconscious go to work. I carry a pen and notepad wherever I go and jot down notes if I see or hear or read something that might fit into a sermon. I find that if I wait until the week before I preach to think about the sermon, I may miss out on a lot of useful material.

A few weeks before preaching I haul out the books and get down to serious study and reading. I do all of my sermon work at home because I have to be alone with no interruptions. When I'm in my office at the church, I like to have my door open for anyone who needs me, which means I can't do anything that requires sustained concentration. I try to block out at least one morning a week for sermon work.

First I pray. I ask God to guide and work through me so that the sermon will do three things: glorify God, speak to the needs of the congregation and challenge them to deeper commitment and service. I make copious notes on the computer and compose a first draft. This draft is completed a few weeks ahead of time, then is set aside until about five days before I preach. At this point I do a lot of editing and usually end up with several more drafts. I add or take away material according to what is happening in the church or the world during that week. I mentally make those changes up to the moment I preach.

Now the real work begins. How do I make this sermon my own? By practicing it to the point where I no longer need the manuscript. Six years into my ministry, I made a decision to preach without a manuscript or notes. I was an associate pastor at the time and had a good role model in the senior pastor with whom I worked. He had a gift for communicating, in large part because he was not tied to a manuscript and could stand right out in front of the congregation.

For 14 years I've preached most Sunday mornings without a manuscript. It is very difficult work and does not come naturally to me. I need several days to refine a sermon to the point where I can preach it. I believe it's worth all the extra hours, though, because it makes me a much better communicator. In addition to the sermon itself, I usually choose a prayer song to open and close the sermon. This reflects my belief in the saying, "S/he who sings prays twice." By the time Sunday morning rolls around, the sermon is not just something I read. It's a part of who I am. It comes from deep within the heart.

The consequence of this style of preaching is that Saturday evening is the pits. All night I wrestle with the sermon. While the rest of the world is out to dinner, seeing a movie or attending a sports event, I am pacing in the basement. Every Saturday night before I preach, I say to God, *I can't do this! Why did you ever call me to be a preacher, anyway?*

Sunday morning I get up very early and do my last preparation while running in the dark. I'm so focused that I can't think of anything else except preaching. Despite my desire to run away or hide, I put on my robe and stole, pray for God's spirit to speak through me, get a drink and walk quietly into the sanctuary, where God meets me and says, "It's OK, Laurie. You'll do just fine. Remember, it's my word, not yours. You're just the messenger. Relax and speak from your heart."

When Sunday morning is over, I am physically and spiritually exhausted, yet also ecstatic. *We did it! I got through it! And, actually, God, it was pretty awesome. What a privilege to be your voice. Thank you, Jesus.*

* * *

I went to a play tonight called *Run for Your Wife*. It's a British comedy about a man who has two wives. After successfully hiding that fact from both wives, he is finally caught in a web of events that threatens to undo his secret life. He attempts to throw off his first wife by pretending he is gay. Although the entire play is hilarious, many jokes are made specifically about homosexuality. I wondered how a person who was gay or lesbian would feel about the jokes and about the play itself. It made me a bit uncomfortable because I have become a lot more sensitized to homosexuality since moving to Grand Rapids.

I will always be grateful to Ed, who, not long after we arrived at First Church, made an appointment to see me. He said, "I've been attending First Church for a little while. I really like it. I want to join your church. I grew up as a United Methodist, and I love church, especially when we have communion. But you need to know I'm gay, and I have AIDS. Am I welcome here?"

So began a journey for Ed and for me. I walked with Ed through the next 18 months until he died. I got to know his friends, I attended a gay party at the home he shared with his partner and I met his parents. I gave communion to Ed, prayed with Ed and discussed theology with Ed. Most important, I continually reminded Ed that he was a child of God and that God loved him.

On the attendance registration pads that are passed through the pews every Sunday, Ed often wrote these words: "The body of Christ has AIDS." It was a poignant reminder every week that we all have AIDS. Each one of us must struggle with what AIDS means and do all in our power to find a cure.

When Ed put his offering in the plate on Sunday morning, he would always write on the envelope, "Thank you, God." Ed had a way of seeing through his pain and suffering and never blamed God. He was truly grateful for his partner, his family, his friends, for God's love and for life.

Ed battled his illness with intelligence and courage, always keeping his passion for life. Until then I'd had limited contact with gays and lesbians. But Ed was able to open my eyes and heart and and challenge my mind. In the years since, I have attempted to learn as much as I can about homosexuality, knowing that it is a "hot potato" in most denominations.

Three years ago I preached on homosexuality. It was Worldwide Communion Sunday. I wrote six drafts of that sermon, more than I have done for any other sermon. I also asked several friends to read it and give me feedback. Above all, I prayed that God would use me to help the members of my congregation in their struggle with the issue.

During the sermon I said:

> *I know how difficult this issue is for you because it's difficult for me as well. I have heard many of your stories, I have felt your agony, I have experienced your pain and I know your confusion. I'm going to tell you right up front that I do not have any answers. I am a fellow struggler. But I continue to do a lot of reading and listening and praying, and I hope that we'll be able to find our way together, with God's help.*
>
> *When journalist Bill Moyers was researching a television series on creativity, an artist told him, "If you know what you are looking for, you will never see what you do not expect to find. If the grace of God is as extraordinary as we say it is, we should be willing to give surprise a chance." This artist was talking about worship, but his statement can be applied here as well. If we think we already know all there is to know about homosexuality, we'll never be open to the surprising grace of God. Emily Dickinson once wrote, "The unknown is the mind's greatest need, and for it no one thinks to thank God." I trust we will all be open to the unknown and thank God for it.*

Near the end of the sermon, I said:

The things I would suggest are not very concrete because I don't think any of us holds the key to the mystery of homosexuality. We need to keep an open mind. We need to learn how to hold in creative tension the words of the Bible that seem to condemn certain sexual practices and the possibility that God may be revealing new truths to us about homosexuality.

Perhaps we need to recognize that God's love is greater than any of us can even imagine and that it may not be limited to our own ideas of how love should or should not be expressed. And we need to listen to the stories of homosexuals. Love them. Include them in the life of the church. Encourage them to use their gifts in the service of God. And continue to be open to new surprises from God.

Remember, Christianity is a way of life, not a set of beliefs, and it's a way of life that is not characterized by intellectual certainty. To think that Christians have to be certain about everything only encourages us to be narrow-minded. When we have to have a ready answer for every problem, Christians can turn into dogmatic, self-righteous, judgmental people who then are more likely to become racist, sexist, anti-Semitic, homophobic or just plain mean-spirited. As William Sloane Coffin has written, "I pray that the Lord will save all of us from three things: the cowardice that dares not face new truth, the laziness content with half-truth, and the arrogance that thinks it knows all truth."

*Therefore, I vow to allow God the right to a plural-
istic creation. I vow not to deny anyone full access
to the living God because when I do that, I deny
them an essential part of their very being as a creature of God. I vow to show tenderness and care to
all, even when I don't understand everything. I vow
to remain open to God's leading and thank God for
the unknown. Through careful listening and reflection, I vow to move beyond language and actions
that demonize others. I vow to work for the day
when all of God's children can live together in a sin-
gular world community where we can all reach out
and touch each other and communicate with each
other.*

In the three years since I preached that sermon, I continue to be blessed and challenged by gays and lesbians in my
congregation and truly admire their determination to live
a Christian life when it is so difficult. I am humbled by their
openness, patience and encouragement as I continue to grow
in my own understanding. I have also seen a change in our
congregation as we offer classes and other study opportunities related to homosexuality. Because our congregation truly
believes that the grace of God is as extraordinary as we say it
is, we are willing to give surprise a chance.

* * *

I think I am finally loosening up enough to play. Even here,
on Hilton Head, I have been fairly regimented in my daily
schedule because that's my nature. Today, however, I throw
my plans aside and let the Spirit prompt everything I do. I
have begun memorizing Scripture, something I would never
have taken time for at home. During my devotions this morning, I come up with the idea of typing out all the passages I am
learning and laminating them for my Day-Timer.

Then I go out for a run. It's one of the most beautiful days
we've had so far on Hilton Head—around 80 degrees, clear

blue sky, no humidity. When I first get to the beach, two butterflies land on my foot. At least two dozen other butterflies dance around me, as if to say, "Time for recess, Laurie. Time to come out and play! And don't forget to pay attention to my backside." As I run north on the beach, hundreds of orange monarch butterflies head south and fly past my head. Whenever I am on the beach, I can't help but smile. It doesn't get any better.

When I arrive back at the condo, I shower and take off to play golf. The course is virtually empty, so I am able to play by myself at my own pace. It is heavenly. I revel in the beauty around me, the water, the trees, the birds and, yes, the butterflies.

I finish early and decide to take a drive through a nearby town because of its historical significance. Back home, I pick up a new book and read outside for an hour. After making supper and watching the news, I start a second book. I usually have three or four books going at once. I become so engrossed that I have no idea two and a half hours have passed until the phone rings. It's Gary, saying that Garth is interested in coming to Hilton Head this weekend with the girls.

I get online and talk with him and Gary through instant messaging. By that time it's 10:30 p.m., so I go upstairs, read a little more and go to bed. Except for talking with Garth, I would not have done even one of those things had I been at home. I would have put in a 14-hour day at church and then fallen into bed like a zombie. I rather like this life.

God, no matter where I am or what time it is, help me to live in your time.

* * *

I am still trying to get a handle on this idea of playing and recess. I have been pretty good on my renewal leave. I've taken time to play golf, rent movies on videotape, read novels and walk on the beach. But it's difficult to play for the sake of play. I could do it when I was little. It seemed as if I spent every waking hour outside playing. I don't know when I changed. It may have been in the sixth grade, when I moved to a new town and began attending a school with a strong chess program.

Immediately, I picked up the game and began playing in local school tournaments—usually as the only girl. In the beginning, I loved playing. I bought chess books and became a student of the game. My most vivid memories, however, were of the pressure. It was not pressure forced on me by my parents. They never made me play chess.

The stress was self-induced. I have always been a competitive person and have never been satisfied with less than my very best. I felt compelled to win at chess, but to win demanded all the concentration and intellectual power I could muster. I did well at competitive chess until seventh grade when I suddenly dropped out in the middle of the year. Chess simply wasn't fun anymore. It became more than a game.

I may never play chess again. It makes me sad, but that does not concern me as much as my continued inability to play. I do pretty well when I am out of town on vacation. After a few days, I am usually able to put work behind me and relax. I have a real problem balancing work and play at home, though. Play just doesn't happen much, and when I do allow myself to play, I work at it. It's that addiction to work again.

I heard recently that the three most important things in life are work, play and worship, not necessarily in that order. The speaker went on to say that, unfortunately, instead of working at our work, playing at our play and worshiping at our worship, we often work at our play, worship our work and play at our worship. Food for thought. It's clear I am going to have to get a handle on this work and play stuff if I am going to remain healthy and effective in ministry. Fortunately, our two daughters, Sarah and Talitha, are flying in tonight for a long weekend—and they know how to play!

God of Small Doses

Small images here and there of a God who longs to be seen;

God in excellence, God in music, God in people, God in the world;

Whatever you do, do it with your whole heart as best you can.

Signs of the holy are everywhere.

Don't let God pass you by.

Stop. Look. Listen.

Butterflies again—they chase me; my head is a landing strip.

A continual emptying of self makes room for God.

Can I still see God in the midst of long days and a myriad of demands?

Do I work at my play?

Worship my work?

Play at worship?

Maybe there is another way.

Give surprise a chance.

Work at work,

Play at play,

Worship at worship.

Small doses of a God who longs to be seen.

Playing to the glory of God.

CHAPTER 8

Transformation

O Lord, your steadfast love reaches all the way to the heavens and your faithfulness to the clouds.

Your holiness is like a mountain and your judgment is like the depth of the sea.

You love us so much that you save humans and all creatures, O Lord.

How precious is your grace, O God.

You will protect us in the shadow of your wings so that we can feast on your abundance.

You even invite us to drink from the river of your delights.

Because you, O God, are the fountain of life; from your light we see light.

AS I PONDER Psalm 36 this morning, I can only marvel at the wisdom and understanding of the psalmist. I'm also amazed that I can't recall ever reading those words before! Certainly, they did not have the impact that they are having today. As I sit at my computer, I look outside to the heavens and soak in God's steadfast love. I see the wispy clouds and know that God is faithful. A myriad of colorful birds swoops past my window. Four deer stand under a huge oak tree. An alligator suns himself on the bank. A gecko hurries along the deck.

You save humans and animals alike, O Lord.

Four golfers are approaching the 10th green. One is obviously not happy with his shot. Yet, Lord, you take him under the shadow of your wings. Another hooked a shot into the pond 20 feet from where I sit. Yes, Lord, you give him drink from the river of your delights. The morning light is dazzling.

What do I experience all around me? I hear God shouting, pleading, whispering, cajoling, "I'm here. Love me. Love me. Love me." I believe the purpose of the spiritual life is transformation. That's the goal for my renewal leave. By opening myself to God's grace, I want my will, my mind, my heart and my spirit to be transformed. I can't make it happen, though. I have to allow God to transform me. Certainly, I have to say yes. I have to agree to give up my will, and I have to be willing to change. Nevertheless, this transforming grace is a pure gift of God.

How could I not have known that? I chastise myself. I've been in the spirituality business for 20 years. How could I have missed it? The answer is simple. I wouldn't let God give me that gift. I was too busy with my own agenda. I put all my other loves before my love of God. I recalled the time of catharsis several weeks ago. All God wants is for me to accept God's gift of grace and respond in love. Soak in the warmth of God's love and allow myself to be transformed.

It has always been difficult, however, to accept God's love without thinking I have to check a hundred items off my to-do list every day to be worthy of that love. After all, God expects a lot of me and I dare not be lazy. No wasting time with Jesus. Suddenly, the thought comes to me: *I don't let other people help me, either. I'm a very independent sort. It's easy for me to give but very difficult to receive. But the important part is really the receiving, isn't it? It's only by receiving that we are truly able to give.*

I think about my girls. Sarah and Talitha are still sleeping. We arrived home from the airport around 1 a.m. I know they are going to want to go shopping this weekend, and I'm prepared. I am not a shopper, so I'm taking a book along just in case.

I take pleasure in buying things for my children. But the greatest gift I could ever give to them has nothing to do with material things. What they need from me above all else is unconditional love, constant encouragement and my time, energy and guidance in discovering God at work in their lives. They need to know that I will always be there for them.

I can't think of a single material gift that I have given to my children that has made any significant impact on their life. However, I have tried to give them the gift of myself. Countless hours have been spent over the last six years working through difficult family issues. I have gone to every school and sports event that I could. I've helped with homework, walked the mall endlessly, taken them back and forth to college and sat up late at night talking with them. Now two of my children are here with me.

I will give them my undivided attention for the next three days. I will listen to them, laugh, cry, play and commiserate with them. We're going to waste time together. It's the best gift I can think of. Unfortunately, it won't replace shopping, but that's OK. It's OK because 10 years from now my daughters won't remember a single thing they bought here. What they will remember is that we were together.

I hope to give Sarah and Talitha the gift of myself in the next few days. But this time, I will also be open to receiving their gifts to me. My prayer is that we will be for one another the steadfast love of God and the fountain of life and that we will all be transformed.

* * *

"I will praise you with my whole heart." As I meditate on Psalm 138, I admit that I have been withholding part of my heart from God for many years. I have been keeping something back for myself. I cannot let go entirely. Consequently, I am not able to receive God's love in all its fullness.

Thomas Merton writes that many Christians have no idea how immense God's love is for them. Nor are they aware of the capacity of that love to do good and bring them happiness. That has been true for me. I truly had no idea. On this renewal leave, I have been able to fully surrender to God and have felt God's love for me more than ever before. I am continually bathed in the light of God's love, and I feel as if I have much more love for God. I am learning how to love God with my whole heart. The challenge is to keep that love strong when I am back home in the midst of the constant demands of a busy family and church.

I also hope I can convey some of that love to my daughters, especially Sarah. She has struggled with low self-esteem for many years, which has resulted in a variety of self-destructive behaviors. Sarah is such a beautiful young woman with a gorgeous smile, filled with energy, life and vitality. She has grace and class and has shown immense courage in the face of many obstacles.

Sarah loves her family, her aunts, uncles and cousins and especially her grandparents. She is loving and kind toward them and is full of hugs and kisses. She is not afraid to say, "I love you." But Sarah does not often value herself, nor does she have any idea how much God loves her. Until she feels that overwhelming love, I fear she will not get her life together and will continue to struggle.

Gary and I have tried so hard to be there for Sarah. We know that all three children live with the label of "preacher's kid." With them it's even worse because we are both preachers. We do not want to saddle them with unrealistic expectations or demands.

I suspect at times we err on the other extreme. We don't talk constantly about Christianity because we feel it just adds one more layer of stress for them. I think as they get older we will be freer to share faith talk, and they will be more comfortable sharing their questions and doubts.

Lord, let me be a channel of your love to my children.

What a wonderful and a full day! After I finally get the girls going around noon, we go to the outlet stores for three hours, then come back and go to the beach. Finding an elusive starfish is a special treat. We eat dinner at a seafood restaurant so that Talitha can have lobster. Sarah, a vegetarian, even splurges and orders shrimp and pasta. This is the first time I have eaten out since coming to Hilton Head.

The dinner is an especially beautiful time of bonding and conversation. We talk about the courses both girls are taking in school and the possibility of Sarah studying abroad during fall semester next year. I ask them where they see themselves 10 years from now, which elicits interesting conversation about goals, dreams and vocation. There is lots of laughter.

We talk about Garth and lament the fact that he overslept for his most important midterm of the semester. We all feel really bad for him but are glad to hear he can take it next week. Then Sarah mentions how Dad is not doing well at home and that he really misses me. Sarah is a very sensitive young woman and always has been in tune with how people are feeling. Talitha asks, "Mom, what do you actually do all day?" I tell her.

In the evening, we go to the grocery store because the girls need to pick up some personal items. I ask Talitha why she doesn't just get them at home, and she replies, "It's because I always have to go shopping with Dad!" We load up the cart with Toss Lotion, Frizz Control Creme, Moisturizing Body Wash, Skin Firming Lotion, Moisturizing Nail Polish Remover, Skin Sensitive Daily Cleansing Pads, Fresh Styling Water and Extra Strength Nail Protector, all for only $50—a real bargain, I am told. I would never use any of those items myself.

I am so tired that I go to bed at 10 p.m. and wake up at 7:30 a.m. It's the first time in recent memory that I sleep nine and a half hours. After being alone for a month with little conversation with anyone, yesterday was a shock to my system. The day was not physically exhausting as much as emotionally draining. I am simply not used to nonstop talk, but I loved it all. More than anything, I want Sarah and Talitha to be free to share what is in the deepest recesses of their heart. Even though I am very different from both girls, I try very hard not to influence their actions and choices but simply listen and love.

* * *

In the morning, I get the girls out on bicycles, and we ride along the beach for a few miles. Then it's off for a final round of shopping before watching the sunset on the beach. What a gorgeous part of God's earth this is!

In the evening, Sarah and Talitha want to go out, but there isn't whole lot for teenagers to do in Hilton Head in October. I drop them off at Harbour Town and ask them to call me when they want to be picked up. They end up meeting two teenage boys from Wales who are visiting with their parents. They have a marvelous time comparing cultures and learning about each other. Of course, Mom is the bad guy who insists on picking them up at 10:45 p.m.—well before their bedtime but well past mine.

I am rather amazed at how social the girls are. They are very outgoing and make friends easily, which is almost exactly the opposite of me. To be fair to myself, however, I did not come to Hilton Head to make new friends and be social. I came here to live in solitude for five and a half weeks.

After the girls leave for home, I spend the day recovering and marveling. I had a wonderful time with them. They certainly do have minds of their own. It's not fun when we butt heads, but I am counting on the fact that their ability to think for themselves and deal with difficult issues will be a great gift in adulthood. In the end, that's how Christian transformation takes place and new life is born—not through blind acceptance but through wrestling and struggling with our faith in the context of a loving and encouraging church family.

When I go back to First Church, I will begin teaching our seventh and eighth grade confirmation class. This yearlong class meets every Sunday morning with the goal of teaching our youth what it means to be a Christian. We learn about the Bible, the life of Jesus, church history, our United Methodist heritage and our local church. We experience different types of worship through visiting other churches, including a Jewish synagogue.

Our goal in confirmation, as for all of our children, youth and adult programming at First Church, is not to produce cookie-cutter Christians who think and believe exactly alike. We desire to have a faith community that is theologically conversant and spiritually diverse. Therefore, our goal is for young and old alike to understand the basics of Christianity so that they can think theologically, be open to how God speaks to them, come to their own unique faith and develop a passion for serving others in Christ's name. We especially emphasize to our children and youth that there is no such thing as a stupid question and nothing is off-limits for discussion. We want our youth to feel comfortable sharing their deepest fears, doubts, concerns and joys.

Last year, I met individually with each youth shortly before the end of the class. I shared how they will be confirming the faith their parents declared at their baptism and how confirmation is a very important step, but only one step in their journey of faith. They are embarking on a life-long process of learning, growing, serving and loving in Christ's name.

Then I asked if they had any questions or concerns that we did not address in the class. One youth asked how the Christian faith could be reconciled with scientific theories about creation, like the Big Bang theory.

Another youth wondered about a video she saw of missionaries trying to convert non-Christians in another part of the world. The missionaries were claiming that the non-Christians were going to hell if they didn't believe exactly as the missionaries believed. That was scary, the youth said. Do United

Methodists think like that? No, I reassured the teen. Yes, we have missionaries who share their faith in Jesus Christ with people around the world, but they never force their beliefs on anyone else. That's not our way.

Another teen asked hesitantly, "Is it OK if I don't believe exactly the same things that you believe?" I answered, "I sure hope you don't believe exactly like me. If so, then I haven't been a very good teacher."

I shared with them my hope that First Church would continue to be a safe place to wrestle with their faith and become the kind of person God created them to be. I assured them that Gary and I would continue to pray for them during the years to come and that the congregation would also be a support for them. I ended my time with each youth by praying with them and asking God to bless them in the days and years ahead.

Sarah, Garth and Talitha are all products of that confirmation class. They have learned about faith and have also had the opportunity to put their faith into action through service projects, summer work camps and a trip to Cuba to visit our sister church. We are not in the same places on our spiritual journeys. But I trust God to guide and lead them into a future where faith and service will be a central part of their lives.

* * *

God certainly has a sense of humor. As I prepare for a long bicycle ride on the beach this morning, I think to myself, "I'd really like to have another starfish for the girls since we only found one while they were here." Then, as I always do before a run or a bicycle ride, I pray, *God, I'm paying attention. I am open to however you want to show me your backside today.* I head south, toward the end of the island, and after a few minutes, I see a starfish! As I pick it up, a woman walking by says, "If you just keep going, you'll find a lot of starfish." I wonder what she means. After all, I have only found a few starfish in five weeks. And my parents, avid beachcombers, have never found any starfish in the 15 years they've been coming to Hilton Head.

In a matter of seconds, my mouth drops open and I stare in amazement. The beach is littered with starfish! Some have one or more arms broken off, but most are perfect. I laugh out loud and say, *God, I only asked for one! Now what am I going to do?*

Starfish washed onto the beach by the tide are dying, so it won't do any good to throw them back into the ocean. Surveying the scene, I decide that perhaps I can pick up enough starfish to give one to all the children in the church as part of our children's time during worship some Sunday. I gather around 70 starfish, rinse them off and prepare to put them in the basket on the back of my bicycle.

That's when my plan falls apart. Because the sand is soft, the kickstand doesn't hold, my bicycle falls over, the basket flies off, and the three dozen starfish I already have in there are thrown onto the sand, some breaking off arms. The basket had only been precariously attached to the bicycle and needed fixing, but I thought my temporary solution of using twist ties to secure the basket was clever. I am wrong. The twist ties have disappeared, and there is no way to attach the basket.

Here I am with 70 starfish in a basket three miles from home. I try to hold the basket with one hand while the other hand steers the bicycle, but the basket is too heavy. The only solution is to delicately balance the basket in the center of the handlebars. I wrap my thumbs around the basket with the other fingers steering. It works for half a mile until the front tire catches on the edge of the bike trail and my starfish and I tumble into someone's front yard. I methodically put all my starfish back into the basket, noting that at least 15 more arms have been amputated in the accident and left at the scene. I carefully get back on the bicycle and ride home without further incident. After dealing with the greatest physical challenge of my renewal leave, I notice that at least half of the starfish now have missing limbs.

I believe God works in and through all the events in our lives. Most of the time, however, we pass right by God's backside without even noticing. We're either too busy to see God, distracted by other things or not willing to open our hearts to receive God's love.

I decide that the basket represents my ministry. I often carry a heavy load. I think I have to bear the burdens of the entire congregation on my own shoulders and be all things to all people. In his book, *Open Secrets; A Spiritual Journey Through a Country Church*, Richard Lischer quotes a friend who says that most Protestant ministers are a "quivering mass of availability"—implying that our ego drives us to put our personal stamp on everything and be there for everyone at all times so that our own need to be needed is fulfilled.

I confess that I am often that quivering mass of availability, needing to be there for my quivering mass of starfish that represent the human hurts and hopes of my congregation. Some starfish are whole, but most are broken in some way. It's the same with my parishioners. When I try to carry their burdens myself, it's like trying to balance the basket on my bicycle. It's impossible. I can do it for a while, then I stumble and fall. I gather up all the burdens and try again. Sooner or later, however, I will fall again because the load is simply too heavy. When I fall, even more limbs are broken.

It's a wonderful image for the shape of my ministry over the last 20 years and why I have needed this renewal leave. God is the bicycle. For years, I proudly rode off to the beach without making sure the basket of my ministry was firmly connected to the bicycle. I have not allowed God to walk with me and share the burdens. I vainly thought I could do it myself—that I should be able to do it myself. It's just another example of how disconnected I have been from the source of life and love.

The starfish are now lying out to dry. I hope I have enough for the children. Some will probably have to take home a broken starfish. I know that won't be their first choice. To be broken is never anyone's choice. But I did find a special starfish to show them. It has an arm broken off, but a new one was starting to grow back. I hope I can share with them about how, when we are broken, Jesus can heal us. All we have to do is keep our basket connected to the bicycle.

* * *

I have decided to fast today until sundown. Fasting is a spiritual discipline with which I have little experience other than giving up candy and desserts for Lent, something I've done for years. I do believe that the absence of food can draw us closer to God. I've had a sweet tooth my entire life, so giving up desserts is extremely difficult. Every day I am sorely tempted to cave in, yet the knowledge of Christ's sacrifice on the cross reminds me that I, too, can learn to sacrifice—even if in a much smaller way. I truly feel as if I am journeying with Jesus through Lent by forgoing desserts.

In fasting, we give up what controls us in order to move in a new direction. We voluntarily deny our physical appetites to engage in a spiritual activity. The hunger pangs are a call to seek God in a deeper way. I toyed with the idea of fasting earlier in my leave but decided against it because I thought the lack of food would dull my mind and render me virtually incapable of writing, reading or focusing on God. My excuse was that the spiritual discipline of fasting was not what I needed at the moment.

I think I've changed my mind, especially after reading what others have written about the joys of fasting. Today is the day. I think I'd like to go 24 hours without food but then decide on a compromise. Since it is new to me, I'll settle for fasting until sundown if I feel I cannot go on any longer.

Fasting needs to have a spiritual focus. It's not a matter of going about life as usual with the exception of eating. Otherwise, fasting becomes simply an exercise in willpower, a show of holiness or a way to lose weight. The purpose of my fast is to seek God in a deeper way.

Some people broaden the meaning of fasting. Giving up something can include more than food. We can give up criticizing other people, speaking too quickly or losing our temper. The idea is to identify something that is getting in the way of our relationship with God and vow to work on it. During the course of the day, when we find ourselves tempted in that specific way, we are prompted to turn in another direction.

During Lent, we preachers sometimes even suggest adding something for Lent rather than giving up something. That addition could range from attending a Bible study, doing daily devotions, working in a soup kitchen once a week, visiting people in nursing homes or finding one person every day and doing something nice for them.

Fasting as a spiritual discipline, however, is also a physical discipline and revolves around food. When I awake this morning, I feel hunger pangs and have a slight headache. Not a good omen. I am eager to pursue my goal, to seek God in a deeper way. Upon further prayer reflection, I decide my goal really should be to allow God to find me in a deeper way.

I go out for a nine-mile run this morning along the beach. I am curious to see if there are more starfish in the same place. Sure enough, they're still there—not many, but they're there. This time I let them be. It's another gorgeous day—warm, breezy, with a few clouds here and there. I am in the middle of my daily routine, praying individually for members of our staff, my family and those prayer concerns of which I am aware. Suddenly, I see a sand dollar along the edge. The only other sand dollar I found during these six weeks broke in my pocket, so I was hoping to find at least one to take home.

A wonderful Christian legend about the birth and death of Jesus has arisen around the sand dollar. If you examine a sand dollar closely, you'll see five holes, which represent four nail holes in Christ's hands and feet and a fifth hole made by a Roman spear. On one side, you see an Easter lily—in the center of which is the star that appeared to the shepherds in Bethlehem. On the other side of the sand dollar is etched the Christmas poinsettia. Finally, if you break open the center of the sand dollar, you will find five white doves waiting to spread peace on Earth.

As I pick up the sand dollar, I have visions of sharing this story with children in the church. Imagine my surprise, then, when I turn over the sand dollar and discover the front is encrusted with tiny shells! I laugh out loud and say: *Another surprise, God! You are showing me your backside again.* That sand dollar is now an even more powerful symbol of Christ, for the encrusted shells are the burdens that Jesus promises to carry for us.

It's now 9:30 p.m. and I decide to wait until tomorrow to eat. It will have been a 36-hour fast. Early afternoon was the worst time for me. It took all my willpower to keep going. After a while, though, I didn't even feel particularly hungry. It almost felt like being in a "zone" while running. You exist on a different level than the rest of the world. I felt very much at peace the whole day and believe that I will try fasting again. I am not afraid of it anymore because I know that with God's help I can do it!

Postscript: I awake at 3 a.m. so hungry that I cannot sleep, so I go downstairs and have some cereal. How is it, I think, that we can allow millions of children in this world to go to bed hungry every single day?

* * *

This is my last full day in Hilton Head. For five and a half weeks, I have lived in solitude. Except for the three days when Sarah and Talitha were here, I have had virtually no direct contact with other people. I did talk with family members on the phone on occasion and had email contact with a few selected family and friends.

I have tried to focus on simply loving God and allowing Christ to master me, to transform me into his likeness. Now, as I move on in my physical and spiritual journey, several things will stay with me. I will remember kind words and deeds, mostly from people I didn't know.

One morning while jogging I passed a mother and two little children on bicycles. The younger one, about 3, said to her mother, "Look, Mom, she's a great runner! I want to run just like that." It doesn't take any more than that to make my day.

Last week, I was crossing a golf cart path on my run and an elderly man said to his buddy, "Let's let her pass." Then he said to me, "You've got a good stride going!"

"Thank you!" I said with a smile.

A few days later, four men in a golf cart saw me running, and one man said, "You're doing just great. Three miles to go!"

I said, "Thanks!"

This week, while golfing, a man playing on another hole saw me and yelled, "Hey! A left-handed girl! I love it!"

Just minutes ago, near the end of my run, a couple on bicycles passed me. The man said to me, "It's been discouraging. We've been pedaling like hell and couldn't catch up to you. You've got a good pace going."

I said, "Thanks!"

When the girls were with me, we pulled up to a tollbooth, and the man working there said, "You're free to go. The man four cars ahead of you paid for the next four cars."

One day, out of the blue, my father sent me a dozen roses. The card said, "No special event. Just because it's you. Love, Dad."

People seem friendlier here than at home. Perhaps it's because most folks on Hilton Head are either retired or on vacation. They're not as hurried, are more relaxed and are kinder to one another. Or it could be that I am not as hurried and am more relaxed here. Thus, I am able to notice the kindness of others. It reminds me how little acts of love and care can make a great difference.

I will also remember the kindness that has been shown to my family while I've been gone. It is impossible for Gary to fill in for me as a mother and as a pastor at the church. He has his own role to play as father and pastor. He has done admirably well, but he can't be in two or three places at once. Many people in the church have given rides to our children, taken them shopping, gone with them to appointments and brought food over to the house. They have visited people in the hospital, made phone calls, taught classes and taken care of a myriad of the details of ministry.

When I think of the adjustments so many people have had to make for me to be gone for three months, my first temptation is to feel guilty, as if I've been incredibly selfish. But just when I am feeling that way, I receive an email or a letter affirming my leave and, in essence, telling me, "You go, girl!"

I will remember being very close to God. I have been given the gift of time and space to become reacquainted with myself and with God. I have been stripped of everything that has given me identity in life. Here on Hilton Head, I am not a mother, I am not a wife, I am not a daughter, I am not a friend, I am not a pastor. I am simply Laurie, child of God. Not receiving any of the affirmation and strokes that go along with those roles was painfully difficult at first. I had to become completely empty, however, in order to free myself for God.

I cannot fully know myself until I know God, for we humans are made to be in communion with God. There is a longing in everyone for God, something instinctive within that wants to be godly. We are infused with the breath of God. That's what it means when the creation story in Genesis says that we are made in the image of God. We do have a capacity for righteousness and holiness, but too often we never reach that capacity for God. Call it sin, rebellion, separation, self-centeredness. Call it what you will. The sad truth is that much of the time we fall short of our divine potential. By allowing Jesus to take apart my life sin by sin and put it back together with grace, I have begun to enlarge my capacity for God.

The Westminster catechism says that the "chief end" of humans is that we "glorify God and enjoy God forever." That phrase was always a mystery to me. I never took the time to glorify and enjoy God. I thought it was selfishness and narcissism. Now I understand that by loving God more, I will be able to love others better. As Thomas Merton has written in *Thoughts in Solitude*, I hope to replicate the balance and perfection that I see in the character of Jesus in my own unique way.

I have only begun the journey toward spiritual maturity, however. Today I am meditating on Mark 8 where Jesus fed 4,000 people with seven loaves of bread and a few fish. Afterward, Jesus and the disciples got into a boat to go to the other side of the Sea of Galilee. There, Jesus was met by the Pharisees, who began arguing with him. Jesus tired of the debate, so he and the disciples got back into the boat and went to the other side again. The disciples realized they had forgotten to bring any bread. They only had one loaf, so when Jesus began talking about the danger of the leaven of the Pharisees, they thought he was referring to their lack of bread. Jesus chided them, saying: "Why are you talking about having no bread? Don't you get it? Are your hearts hardened? You have eyes yet fail to see? You have ears yet fail to hear? Don't you remember? … Don't you understand?" (Mark 8:17-18)

Don't you yet understand? In so many ways, I do not yet understand the mystery of God. I still don't trust that God will supply all my needs, including bread. I still don't always see God's backside. I still don't always hear God's voice calling my name. I still become distracted during my prayer time. I still resist allowing the Spirit to master me. I am still reluctant to welcome the transformation God wants to work in me. I still resist going out for recess. Yet I also believe Thomas Merton when he writes that the more content we are with our own poverty, the closer we are to God. He says that is because when we are at peace with our poverty we don't expect anything from ourselves but everything from God.

Lord, I confess that I still don't always understand. I accept my poverty of spirit in peace and rest in your mercy.

A last learning I will take with me is a deeper realization that our lives on earth are more important than we even comprehend. Nothing that I do in this renewal leave can be called spiritual if it does not help other people become more faithful servants in the world. When I read the descriptions of judgment in the Gospels, it's clear that they speak almost exclusively of the deeds people have done. After accepting God's gracious gift of Jesus Christ, we are called and, indeed, empowered to fulfill God's purposes in the world.

My goal when I reenter active ministry is to help people reach their divine potential, to remind them that they are made in the image of God and that God wants to be a part of their life. I want to foster a sense of openness and acceptance so that all people feel welcomed and loved wherever they are in their spiritual journey. Sure, it would be nice to stay here. No stress, lots of sun, freedom, time to play and stay close to God. But that's not enough. I am convinced that God has more in store for me.

Light of the world, lead me to you.

A Prayer for My Children

Given to me as a gift but not mine.

Charged to love and nurture into adulthood, trying to reflect your steadfastness.

Amazed at their wisdom and maturity;

Young as they are, I learn from them;

Battered to and fro by the challenges of adolescence and undeserved tragedy;

May my continual tears protect them from harm.

Curious to know where they will be 15 years from now,

I wonder, pray and hope;

Strengthened by God's grace to be a constant source of love, tough or tender,

I will be there for them.

Blessed by the privilege of mothering, we lock arms and walk into the future.

With generous hearts for the poor, the oppressed, and downtrodden,

for all those who are rejected, for whatever reason;

Their compassion shames my hypocrisy.

Humbled

Chastened

Awed

By my children.

Kayaking in Hilton Head.

CHAPTER 9

On the Road

ON THE ROAD again! I drive from Hilton Head to Asheville, North Carolina, where I spend a day with a dear friend from First Church. Then I have a 12-hour drive from Asheville to Grand Rapids. It's interesting how road trips to a destination are a lot easier than the drive back home. You're so excited about leaving town and getting away that the drive is actually fun! But, coming home, the feelings are very different. At least for me they've always been. I almost always have a great time on vacation and don't want to leave. If I have to come home, I want to get there as fast as I can. At the same time, I dread getting back into the same old routine. Of course, my renewal leave isn't over, so I'm not reentering pastoral life immediately, but I'm still going back to my home and my family.

I become bored after several hours on the road, so I turn on the radio to see what is out there. Actually, I know what's out there. That's why I don't listen to the radio very often.

Did you know that, for a contribution to a certain pro-life radio station, you can receive a "feet pin," which is the actual size of a baby 10 weeks after conception? Sorry, they're out of gold, only silver feet pins remain.

I'd never heard of a station like "The Trading Post," where people call in and advertise items they have to sell. A black tool box for a small pickup truck, five birdcages, a 1969 cookbook from a local United Methodist Church, a knife collection, brick-red house paint and an electronic training collar for dogs are all available for a price.

Sports radio is alive and well in America. The dilemma of the day is whether Michael Jordan and the Washington Wizards will draw more television viewers tomorrow night than the World Series between the Arizona Diamondbacks and New York Yankees.

Channel Ford salutes America and reminds listeners that the owner of the car company is a 20-year veteran of the armed forces. They want us to know that we can save thousands by buying a Ford and we'll keep America moving at the same time.

I hear the press conference where Richard Myers, chairman of the Joint Chiefs of Staff, and Donald Rumsfeld, secretary of defense, give an update going into the fourth week of the war in Afghanistan. Afterward, talk radio has a field day. Some people feel that we are moving too quickly and are endangering and even killing innocent people. The predominant opinion, however, is expressed by one man who says, "The media has a pro-Afghan stance. A pox on them all! Something's wrong when we care about women and children of the enemy." Another says, "I'm getting fed up with the peaceniks and media who think we should not be at war."

On Christian talk radio, a woman calls in and wonders what to do because her husband is "backsliding." When the three male hosts reminded her of the Bible's call to "submit" to her husband no matter what (from Ephesians 5), I realize it's time to turn off the radio. I've had enough.

Talk radio is a uniquely American phenomenon. Where else do people have the opportunity to let their voice be heard? Where else do people have the freedom to be as bigoted, offensive and outrageous as they want? It's amazing how many talking heads are on the airwaves. We humans do love to hear the sound of our own voices, don't we? We love to make a point—to put in our two cents. There's an unbelievable smorgasbord of junk out there, but folks love it! One woman was gushing to her favorite radio host yesterday, "I plan all my errands in the afternoon so I can be in the car and listen to your show." My response: *get a life.* As with the information superhighway and television, it's OK that I don't know what's out there because it's often not much.

* * *

It sure feels strange walking into my house after having been gone for almost six weeks. How things can change! Talitha has rearranged the basement. The milk carton now has a new label. There are blue towels in the bathroom. A skywalk has been built over a nearby highway. The high school Fine Arts Center is taking shape. The neighborhood house under construction is almost done. The leaves are gone from the trees. Michigan is settling in for another dreary, cloudy, cold winter. But I'm home, and it feels good.

I often think about what home is. I really felt at home on Hilton Head for the five and a half weeks I was there. It was just God and me, but it was home. And when my girls came to visit, I was proud to share my home with them. In our church, we house homeless families in our building four weeks out of the year. These families call our church home, if only for a week at a time. What makes a good home, anyway? Food, shelter, a warm bed? Yes, they are all important. But a good home also provides a safe, loving, caring and accepting atmosphere.

I rented a video a few days ago, *Where the Heart Is.* I'd wanted to see it for some time because I enjoyed the book by Billie Letts. *Where the Heart Is* tells the story of a 17-year-old teenager, Novalee Nation, and her search for home. Abandoned by her family in Tennessee and discarded by her boyfriend in Sequoyah, Oklahoma, Novalee ends up pregnant and homeless with just $7.77 in her pocket. She gives birth in a Walmart.

In one of the first scenes of the book, a woman in Sequoyah befriends Novalee. When she asks Novalee if she is coming back home to Oklahoma, Novalee says that Oklahoma is not exactly home—but she might stay for a while.

The woman says, "I think that's good. 'Cause home gives you something no other place can. You know what that is?"

"No, ma'am."

"Your history. Home is where your history begins. My late brother used to say, 'Home is the place that'll catch you when you fall. And we all fall.'"

Novalee discovered that the actual location and style of a house is not what makes a home. Home is where you are loved and cared for. Home is where you are accepted whether you deserve it or not. Home is where you are always welcome.

Robert Frost penned these famous words in his poem, *The Death of the Hired Man*, "Home is the place where, when you have to go there, they have to take you in. I should have called it something you somehow haven't to deserve."

Home is the place that'll catch you when you fall. And we *all* fall. That's what Gary and I want our home to be like. We want the doors of our home to always be open because there is only one way to learn how not to fall. That is to receive the love of those who are willing to catch you when you do fall.

That's also the kind of home I hope our church can become. For we *all* fall. On life's journey we'll trip, stumble and occasionally head off in a wrong direction. But the good news is that when we come back to our history, there will be strong hands ready to pick us up, warm arms aching to embrace us and loving hearts ready to take us in. If the church will not pick us up, shake the dirt off our clothes and set us on the right path, who else will?

Grand Rapids is home to me. Elmwood Street is home to me. First Church is home to me. I have a deep sense that this is where I belong, this is my history, this is where I am called to serve and this is where I am loved. There is no other place I'd rather be.

* * *

Today is Halloween. I have warm memories growing up about Halloween. That was in the era of 5-cent candy bars, so my brothers, my sister and I really loaded up on Halloween. When we got home, we'd spread out all our candy on the floor, count the number of pieces, then put the candy in order: all the M&M's, Snickers, Reese's Cups, Milky Ways, Three Musketeers and Hershey Bars would lie together. The Almond Joys and Mounds we gave to my father because none of us liked coconut.

Our children have continued that tradition. They compensated for my inadequacy in the costume department, put together their own outfits and would literally run from house to house in order to get as much candy as they could. When they were young, one of us would go out with the children and the other would stay home and hand out candy. Halfway through the evening, we'd switch. Eventually, they were old enough to go out on their own, so Gary and I could stay home and meet all the ghosts, witches, goblins and angels.

Some Christians don't believe in Halloween, claiming that it celebrates evil and witchcraft. Gary and I take a more casual attitude, allowing our children to have some fun but encouraging positive costumes. Besides, they know that Halloween is connected with All Saints' Day, which celebrates all of the saints who have died in Christian faith. At this time of year, we do not celebrate the power of evil but the power of Jesus to overcome evil and bring resurrection and new life to those who have died.

My most vivid Halloween memory took place on our first Halloween in Grand Rapids. Our children were in second, fifth and seventh grade, prime years for Halloween fun. It was Saturday night and the hours for trick or treating were from 6 to 8 p.m. At 5:30 p.m., we received a frantic call from the hospital. A baby from the church was just diagnosed with meningitis and was in serious condition. Could one of us come up right away?

Gary and I looked at each other. We knew someone had to go, but how would we work out Halloween? We decided that I would go to the hospital and Gary would take the three children. We'd just shut up the house while I was gone and not give out any candy.

I was hoping to get back in time to meet Gary at a certain place so we could at least have a few moments to enjoy Halloween as a family. I rushed to the hospital, not knowing what to expect. I had not met this family yet, but the parents were obviously very shaken and worried. I parked my car in the hospital lot and walked briskly out to the street. The light was yellow, but I didn't see any cars coming. I decided to take a chance and run across the street.

Out of nowhere a pickup truck raced over the hill just as the light turned green and hit me. I was thrown into the air, flipped over and landed on a narrow strip of grass along the side of the street. The driver stopped and called out, "Are you OK?" I was stunned but said, "Yes." He drove off and I got up.

Miraculously, it didn't seem as if anything was broken. I continued walking into the hospital but was in a complete daze. Somehow I made it to the baby's room, met the parents, talked for a while and prayed for the baby. I didn't tell them anything about the accident, but all I could think of was what had just happened. I wondered: *Will the police find me and ticket me for running in front of a truck? Will the driver report what happened? Should I report what happened? Am I really OK?*

I left the hospital after an hour and drove back home where I found Gary and the children happily walking from house to house. I said nothing. I now know that I was in shock. Late that night, I could not sleep. I was frightened that I might have internal injuries of which I was not aware. I was afraid I would get into trouble for not reporting the accident. I imagined all sorts of dreadful scenarios.

In the middle of the night I was at wits' end. I woke Gary and told him what happened. He simply held me and told me not to worry, that everything would be all right. I slept fitfully for a few hours, and in the morning I woke up hardly able to move. My entire body was sorer than it had ever been in my life, but I was OK.

I believe the greatest miracle of my life occurred on Halloween night in 1993. By all rights, I should have been killed. The truck hit me head on at a fast rate of speed. When I flipped, I landed on my side on a tiny patch of green. Everything else around me was concrete.

For years, I avoided that intersection by entering the hospital from a skywalk connected to the parking garage. Today, I can walk across the street, but I'm extremely cautious and will never take a chance like that again.

God was with me that night. That's why I hold no stock in the so-called power of Halloween evil. Because Jesus died on a cross and rose from the dead, the power of evil has been overcome. By God's grace I did not become one of the saints in heaven that night, a saint whose life would be remembered the next morning on All Saints' Day. No, I am still here on this earth. I vowed that weekend to make every moment count, to appreciate each day and to live out my call as best I can.

* * *

The day after Halloween is All Saints' Day. We have a tradition in our church of honoring those who died during the past year. We do it on either the Sunday before or after All Saints' Day. All Saints' Sunday is probably my favorite Sunday of the church year because it gives me a chance to remember and celebrate the lives of people whom I loved dearly and are now living as saints in the presence of God.

Since I've been gone, three of the people I expected would die during my renewal leave did indeed die, all about the same time. I know Gary did a fine job at the funerals, but I regret not being there. Officiating at funerals is one of the most fulfilling aspects of my ministry. It is a time when people are usually very vulnerable and thus receptive to receiving the comfort and hope that Jesus offers to all people. Out of the several hundred funerals I have performed, I have without fail found evidence of grace and much to celebrate in the life of each person who has died. In addition, I have an opportunity to minister to people who would never come to a Sunday morning worship service.

The most agonizing funerals are for babies, children and teenagers or where someone has committed suicide. The most sensitive funerals are for people who were professed non-Christians or where family members are fighting. It's very difficult to officiate at a funeral where I am not allowed to make any references to Jesus Christ or where there is disagreement on what exactly I can say about the person. The easiest funerals are for saints of the church who lived long, good and faithful lives.

Four particular funerals stand out in my mind. In the first, I was doing a funeral in the sanctuary for someone without a close connection to the church. A relative of the person who died was to be the soloist. We decided on three songs over the phone and arranged for her to practice with the organist an hour before the service. When she finally showed up 20 minutes before the service, the organist and I gave each other "the look." The soloist was wearing a purple low cut blouse and the tightest, shortest black miniskirt imaginable. She said, "Where's the music? Let's practice."

"I don't have your music. You picked it out," said the organist.

"Whenever I sing somewhere, they always have the music. It's in the Catholic song book," she replied.

"I don't have a Catholic songbook. This is a United Methodist Church."

"Oh."

We gave her two options: sing without accompaniment or pick several songs from the hymnal and wing it. Fortunately, a bagpipe player was doing the prelude, so they had 10 minutes to whip something together. It's clear she was very nervous, but her solos went OK.

To top it off, our sound man told me after the service that a relative sitting in the front row had a small portable TV set and was watching the Michigan State-Ohio State football game during the funeral. From now on, I guess I'll have to say, "And now, in preparation for worship, will you please turn off all cell phones, pagers, radios, TV sets, video games and computers, put your seat back to its upright position and fasten your seat belt!"

I performed a funeral one time for a man from our church. It was at 10 a.m. Saturday at a local funeral home and I had a wedding at noon at the church. Since we were driving to the cemetery after the funeral, I made sure the funeral directors knew of my timetable. We would have been in good shape if this dear man's large family had not remained weeping in front of the casket for a half-hour after the service. Consequently, the funeral procession had to move along much faster than normal that day.

We arrived at the cemetery at 11:40 a.m., I finished at 11:50 a.m., then drove off as fast as was appropriate under the circumstances. I was in constant contact by cell phone with our building supervisor, who had my robe and microphone waiting for me in the lobby. I walked in the door of the church with 30 seconds to spare just as the bride was set to walk down the aisle.

One of the most beautiful experiences I have had with death occurred a few years ago when a woman in my church died after a two-year struggle with cancer. I had the privilege of walking with Jo the last several months. She asked me to visit two times a week, and every time I went, it seemed as if she ministered to me rather than the other way around.

I had not been particularly close with Jo before she had cancer. In fact, I was rather intimidated by her. She was a hard worker in the church and was involved in many activities, but she also had definite ideas.

It was amazing how Jo and I came to dearly love each other during those last months. I still remember how stunned I was when she called me her friend for the first time. When she said, "I love you," I melted.

Jo used her illness as an opportunity for personal and spiritual growth, and I saw great changes in her. She decided to embrace the cancer, to become vulnerable and give up the control she loved so dearly. She opened up more than she ever had before. She struggled with difficult questions in an honest, searching way, and I saw her become more and more willing to accept the help and care that others offered.

Jo asked me to compile a list of scriptures that would be comforting to her. I went through the list whenever I visited, and we would always close by saying Psalm 23 together. Jo's two young adult daughters cared for her at home right up to the end, and her husband was by her side as much as he could be. She talked in detail about her memorial service and gave me this warning, "Don't make me out to be a saint!"

On the afternoon Jo died, she had not really responded since the night before. Shortly before she died, however, Jo whispered her last words, the same words she had faithfully said to her family and friends for months now, "I love you." A short time later, Jo opened her eyes and smiled. Her whole face lit up, changed and became more peaceful. It was as if she'd just run into a hundred of her closest friends.

Her daughter asked, "Did you see the light?"

"Yes," Jo whispered.

I believe Jo was saying to her family, "It's OK here in heaven. It may need a little organization, but we'll get this place whipped into shape. Don't worry about me. I have fought the good fight, I have finished the race, I have kept the faith. Never forget, I love you."

Several years ago, I had the privilege of officiating at the funeral of a retired pastor in our congregation. I had met Jim's extended family several years before when Jim's wife died. Even though Jim's sons and their families live far away from Michigan, I felt an immediate bond that was renewed when I met them again. After the funeral, a daughter-in-law came up to me and said, with a tinge of regret, "I don't think I will ever see you again."

I have discovered that I get to know people rather quickly at the time of a funeral. The relationship is an intimate one, sharing from the depths of our hearts about the person who died, talking about family and church and what is important in life. I told Susan that it was an honor to meet Jim's family. I said that one of the wonderful things about life is the people we meet only once or twice but who have a significant impact upon us and are examples of God's incredible grace. I thank God for:

- The person who stopped and helped when I had a flat tire.
- The older man I met while traveling as a teenager in England who bought me dinner on a train in which we were riding.
- The nurse who was so compassionate when we were in the emergency room for one of our children's many accidents.
- The visitor to First Church, just passing through town, who expressed kind words of appreciation for the church and its warmth.
- The clerk at the checkout counter who remained unflappable and gracious when harassed by impatient shoppers.

- The stranger who slowed down to run with me during the last painful miles of my first marathon and talked me through it.
- The tour guide who made a trip so much fun.
- The people from other countries that our family has been host to over the years and who have been a source of true delight.
- The doctor who knew exactly what to do when I had a severe allergic reaction to a medication.

I recently read that only a handful of people, perhaps four or five, really make a long-term difference in our life. I tend to agree. But I am equally grateful for the people God sends to us every day—those who enter our life but for a moment and then disappear, whose names we never know and who may touch us only once but do it in a profound way. Thank God for all those who pass in and out of our lives and for the example of grace they are. I would call them saints.

* * *

The day is here, and I wake up anxious. Gary left early for the hospital to be with someone who was having heart bypass surgery, and once more feelings of uselessness and emptiness invade my serenity. It is so much more difficult to detach myself from the life of the congregation when I am in town. I've tried. I decide not to answer the phone while I am home alone this week. One time I had to go to the church to take care of a few things, but I went early in the morning so as not to run into anyone.

Last night, I had a meeting with the couple whom I will be marrying the day I return from renewal leave. When I arrived at their house, I thought, "I don't want to be doing this. In fact, I'm not sure I ever want to do this again." But we had a great time together and I left remembering how satisfying ministry usually is.

I know it's difficult for Gary to have me around and not be working because his plate is so full. He is the one who usually complains that I work too hard and don't take time to play. I just finished a book, *Big Stone Gap*, where Ave Maria, the main character, is visiting her ancestral home in Italy. She notices how casual and more laid back life is in Italy. But she also sees her aunt working all the time, so she asks another aunt, "Isn't she going to stay and have some fun?" The reply came back, "She likes to do her chores."

That's me.

I like to do my chores, and I've done a lot this week. I've done the wash, paid bills, made appointments for the children, driven Talitha around, shopped and packed for my trip. At the beginning, it was awkward being home. We sort of tiptoed around each other wondering how the last six weeks may have changed us as individuals and as a family.

The dynamics of the family change radically when one of us is not "pulling our weight," which is how I feel when I am home but not doing my share of ministry. There is really no solution other than talking about it and trying to understand where the other is coming from.

I haven't slept well all week and have had a dull headache, which is very unusual for me. On the one hand, I will be glad to leave again because it's too difficult to be home and not be on the job. I'm also very excited about going to Taizé. On the other hand, I'm more nervous than usual about flying right now, and I worry about my inability to speak French.

Certainly, I do not feel as close to God here as I did on Hilton Head. One morning I'm not even able to do my devotions because of a family matter that came up at the last minute. I sigh and pray: *Is this how it's going to be every day? Always something coming up? Things beyond my control taking time away from you? How can I detach myself from the frenetic pace in order to remain close to you, God?*

Yesterday, when I was out for my run, I lamented to God how dreary and yucky the weather was and how running in the city isn't the same as running along the beach. I prayed: *God, how am I going to find you here in Grand Rapids? How can I allow you to master my spirit and preserve a calm and peaceful heart in the midst of a life filled with demands and distractions?* A few seconds later I heard some loud chirping. A bright red cardinal was perched on the branch of a small bush just yards away. It was as if God was speaking to me, "Pay attention, Laurie. I'm everywhere if only you remember to look and listen for me."

I know it's going to take time to adjust to a new way of living and being. Perhaps I'm being too impatient.

God, please be with me as I make my pilgrimage to Taizé. I am completely open to you.

I am leaving tonight for France.

For All the Saints

Where would I be without the saints?

The great cloud of witnesses that cheers me on.

Nurturing and guiding me, modeling what a Christ-like life looks like.

My beloved grandmothers, Mary and Martha, reminding me of the importance of both action and contemplation.

My mother and father, without whom I would be nothing;

Joan, whose tragic death inspired me to dare to sit on an organ bench and carry on her legacy;

The faithful in my home church, encouraging me, showing me what a faithful life looks like.

The nameless people whose kindness touched me when I was in need.

Why was I so blessed?

How many lives have I touched on my journey?

How will I be remembered?

She was too busy? She never stopped to talk? She didn't know how to let go?

All I want, God, is to love you and bring in your kingdom on this earth for all people.

May I be faithful to you in the one life I have.

More hugs, more smiles, more mentoring, more inspiration;

More of you, less of me.

For all the saints who have gone before and blazed the trail;

A path of wisdom, love, courage, strength and spiritual wisdom.

I mean to be one, too.

Finding God wherever I am.

CHAPTER 10

Darkness and Light

I DON'T SEE it coming. I am totally unprepared—I mean totally—for the feelings I experience after arriving in Paris late Saturday morning. My flight arrives early; I recover my luggage and find a bus to downtown Paris. On the bus I begin to feel extremely anxious. Why am I doing this? I don't want to be here by myself. I remind myself that the reason I am here is to make a pilgrimage to Taizé, not be a tourist. When Gary comes in nine days, then I will be a tourist.

The hotel is quaint. My sixth floor room is very tiny but cute. In a concession to one of my fears, I give in and walk up six flights of stairs with my suitcase. The elevator is extremely small and I cannot bear to increase my anxiety by getting into it.

What am I doing here, halfway across the world? I feel intense loneliness, absolute emptiness and complete disconnection from anything familiar. Before going out to explore, I read through my favorite scriptures. 2 Corinthians 12:9 jumps out at me because I am feeling very fragile, "My grace

is sufficient for you, for power is made perfect in weakness."
I go out for about three and a half hours. It's a beautiful day, and the streets are full of people, but for me there is no joy, no excitement. *I chose to do this?*

As I attempt to discern what's going on inside me, I realize that these are not new feelings. It's almost panic. I felt this way in high school when I visited family friends in Germany. I could not communicate with anyone because I didn't speak German. I didn't know a soul and I wondered why I put myself in that position. The loneliness was a physical pain in the pit of my stomach.

I also had that feeling when my parents took me to Wittenberg University for the first time. I knew no one, I was 10 hours away from home and my three roommates were smoking pot when I found my room. I sobbed as my parents drove off. As a parent, I now know they felt as helpless and sorry as I did.

It was the same when they took me to graduate school at Yale University. I was so scared and unsure of myself that I wanted to hop back in the car and drive home with them. Each time, though, my parents wisely advised me to stick it out for a little while because things would probably get better. And they did. Even though the first few days and weeks were tough, I persevered, and I came to love both college and graduate school.

Never in my wildest dreams did I think I would be flooded with those same feelings today. Here I am—while everyone back home believes that independent, adventurous, confident Laurie is having a grand old time—when in reality I am crying my eyes out.

Certainly, one factor contributing to my state of mind is the language barrier. German and Spanish I can handle, but I don't know any French. I also discover that the stimulation of many people, sounds and cars in Paris is overwhelming, especially after living for six weeks in solitude in a very quiet place. I definitely am not a city person. Gary would attest to the fact that whenever we go to New York City, I get a headache. It's all too much for me.

It is, indeed, a dark day of the soul. I feel totally alone, as if I have been stripped of everything that gives me identity. No one knows where I am, and it seems as if no one even cares where I am. I am completely forgotten. The worst part is feeling disconnected from God.

O God, where are you? Where are you? Why are you so distant? O God, this is unbelievably bad. What is happening? Why is there darkness all around me?

As I admit how weak and vulnerable I feel, I realize how often I look down on the weakness and vulnerability of others. Just yesterday, Sarah had a really bad day, yet when I talked with her I was callous and unsympathetic. Instead of showing compassion, I scolded her. Instead of being understanding, I became angry and listed off all the ways in which she brought her current state of affairs on herself.

Forgive me, Lord. Forgive me, Sarah. I did not know what I was saying.

I felt so good coming home from Hilton Head, close and connected with God, refreshed and renewed. Then, wham! It's like I've totally fallen apart. Clearly, there is more work for God to do in me before I am ready to re-enter ministry. I thought the painful dismantling of my inner life was over, but I guess not.

The unmasking of my true self continues. I am a scared, weak little girl. I've lost sight of the shore again and am drifting in a sea of darkness and despair. All I have to hang on to is the knowledge that deep in the core of my being God loves me. I also take comfort from Henri Nouwen's words in *Making All Things New*, "We must trust that our honesty and courage will lead us not to despair, but to a new heaven and a new earth."

* * *

I am nervous about getting on the right car on the train. Part of the train is going to another city and I want to make sure that doesn't happen. Why do I get so worried about making connections? Perhaps because I missed that train connection in East Berlin 25 years ago and know how easy it is to get messed up. I have to keep reminding myself that the one necessary thing is to love God. Then we are free from the endless causes of worry. For me, however, this will be a process, a long, quiet transformation, just as it had been a long, quiet growing apart from God.

On my run this morning it comes to me again, "One does not discover new lands without consenting to lose sight of the shore for a very long time." Yesterday, I sure lost sight of that shore, but I have to believe that out of it I will discover new lands.

Thank you, God, for bringing me through the night safely.

When I get off the train at Mâcon, a young woman approaches me and asks if I am going to Taizé. She didn't have an opportunity to exchange currencies and needs to borrow some francs for the bus. Marcie and I immediately connect. Clearly, I am very hungry for human contact because we talk the whole hour until the bus comes. It's amazing how she is feeling the same things I am: harried, worried, not centered. I break down at one point and she holds my hand in a wonderfully supportive way.

Marcie is 36 and has been a high school English teacher. She is taking a year off and has come back to Taizé a second time. She does not consider herself a churchgoer at the moment, yet her best friend is an Episcopal priest. She seems to have a good understanding of what I do and keeps saying over and over, "You are so sweet." I was so afraid I would not find anyone with whom to connect at Taizé. As it turns out, she is the only other American there for the week. It is as if Jesus had appeared to me in Marcie.

Thank you, God.

I am fortunate to have a room at the retreat house operated by the Sisters of St. Andrew, an international Catholic community founded 750 years ago. The sisters assume part of the responsibility for welcoming visitors to Taizé.

My first worship service at Taizé is at 5:30 p.m. It is awesome seeing the brothers enter in their white robes. I am struck by how young they look. Brother Roger, the founder of Taizé 61 years ago, is still the prior, but he is 86 years old and seems quite frail. Amazing. I'm glad I came while he was still alive.

My initial impression is that the church looks like a big barn. It's very simply built and the inside is dark, lit by down lights and many candles. There are no chairs. People sit on the floor or use kneelers. My senses are immediately engaged. There is the smell of incense. Large plain red banners hang from the front of the church. Scattered around the church are icons, paintings of scenes from the life of Christ, meant to be focal points for contemplation.

We all have songbooks with numbers projected electronically. The service consists of songs, some with solos or descants, a scripture, a prayer and a 10-minute period of silence. Our worship coincides with our All Saints' service at First Church, which is always very meaningful for me.

At 8:30 p.m., we worship again. The last song we sing would have been perfect for last night, "By night we hasten in darkness to search for living water. Only our thirst leads us onward." I also notice a prayer by St. Augustine, posted inside the door of the church. It speaks powerfully to me after the darkness of the last 24 hours:

Light of my heart, do not let my darkness speak to me! I have drifted to the things of below and have become darkness; but from there, even from there, I have deeply loved you. I have wandered and have remembered you. I heard your voice telling me to come back, but I did not hear properly in the tumult of arguments. And now here I am returning to you burning and panting towards your source. Let no one take me from it. May I drink from it and live from it.

* * *

In 1940, Roger Louis Schutz-Marsauche (Brother Roger), a Reformed minister, arrived in the tiny community of Taizé. He felt that his calling was to a life of prayer and reconciliation. His dream was to live in community with others who wanted to practice the Gospel of Jesus Christ by serving the poor and disadvantaged during World War II in occupied France.

During the war, they helped Jewish refugees escape into Switzerland. After the war, Roger, now a Roman Catholic brother, opened his home to children who lost their parents and fed German prisoners in a nearby camp. Sixty years later, Taizé is an ecumenical community of approximately 100 brothers who have taken vows of poverty and chastity. These brothers come from all over the world and span the entire spectrum of denominational beliefs. The overarching theme of Taizé is justice and reconciliation. At the entrance to the Church of Reconciliation at Taizé are these words:

> *Be Reconciled All You Who Enter Here*
> *Parents And Children; Husbands And Wives;*
> *Believers And Those Who Cannot Believe;*
> *Christians And Their Fellow Christians.*

The focus of Taizé's ministry is with young people, those less than 30 years old. Every summer 3,000 to 5,000 young people make a pilgrimage to Taizé for a week of study, prayer and reflection. They are drawn to the authenticity of faith they find in the brothers and have a deep desire for contemplation and worship. They come to search for meaning, to unlock the key to their inner life and then to leave renewed and empowered to live out their faith in a simple way wherever they are. Taizé's website states: "From its beginning, the community has had a twofold intention: to seek communion with God through personal prayer and the beauty of community prayer, and also to be a leaven of peace and trust in the midst of humanity."

One of the great attractions of Taizé is its unique and simple music, combined with a peaceful serenity and a beautiful location in Burgundy. For many years, the brothers of Taizé worshiped in the tiny village church and from the beginning sang in four-part harmony. They lived out the old saying, "He who sings prays twice."

In the late 1940s, the brothers of Taizé began using Joseph Gelineau's translation of the psalms and his musical settings. In the 1960s and 1970s, when people began discovering Taizé and coming to visit, the brothers had to find a different way to pray so that visitors could more easily participate in worship. Composer Jacques Berthier and Brother Roger worked to develop simple songs that could be sung easily and in many different languages.

With pilgrims arriving from 35 to 70 nations every week, there was a need for music that was global, simple and accessible. Through the use of simple repeated phrases embellished with instrumental music and vocal descants, people are able to participate immediately. The repetition helps to build a relationship with God by freeing the worshippers to pray with the heart while singing.

Pope John Paul II visited Taizé in 1986. He told the young people, "One passes through Taizé as one passes close to a spring of water. The traveler stops, quenches his thirst and continues on his way. The brothers of the community, you know, do not want to keep you. They want, in prayer and silence, to enable you to drink the living water promised by Christ, to know his joy, to discern his presence, to respond to his call, then to set out again to witness to his love and to serve your brothers and sisters in your parishes, your schools, your universities and in all your places of work."

I find the music of Taizé to be quite unique. The refrains are simple and easily learned. The constant repetition not only helps us feel comfortable with the music, but our minds are thus free and we can sing and pray with our hearts. In most churches, when we sing hymns, we may repeat the tune four times, but in each stanza, the words are different. We are sometimes confused and so hung up with getting both the words and the music right that we are not really free to pray the music. Repetition enables us to relax into the familiar and let the spirit move.

At Taizé we are also able to pray with an international community. Though many, we sing with one voice to God. The songs at Taizé are sung in different languages with numerous translations for each song. Even as we sing in a different language, we can understand the meaning in our own language.

I am very aware of how tightly controlled our Protestant services in America are. Time influences our music. We know exactly how long a piece of music is. It has a specific beginning and end. Taizé music, however, has no end. It ends when it ends. The song may be repeated 10, 20 or 30 times. At first, this was disconcerting to me, time conscious as I am. After a while, however, I came to see how Taizé music gives the Holy Spirit the opportunity to act in God's time, not our time. At Taizé, we don't look at our watches. We are praying. We are spending time with God without any agenda.

At Taizé, I am learning to pray with the heart, not the mind. After all, the function of the brain is not to pray but to think. Through the music and silence of Taizé, we allow God to speak to us. It is in silent prayer that we discover our relationship with God and can see God's holiness. I often make the mistake of thinking that my prayers have to be long, articulate theological treatises. Taizé shows me that we need few words to express the depths of our hearts. God doesn't need all the words, and neither do we.

Tonight I sit next to a brother with a beautiful tenor voice. With me singing soprano, we have an incredible duet going. It is a foretaste of heaven for me, one of those ineffable moments I'd like to hold on to forever. We do not know each other and have never met, but our hearts are united in prayer through music.

> *Dare to pray*
> *Dare to sing to Christ*
> *Until you are joyful and serene*
> *By the Holy Spirit*
> *Christ prays in you*
> *More than you imagine.*
>
> *—Brother Roger*

* * *

A week at Taizé is built around the daily rhythm of prayer. Morning prayer is at 8:30 a.m. and consists of a sung psalm, a Scripture read in several languages, several chants, 10 minutes of silence, the Lord's Prayer and communion. We conclude with a few more chants. Midday prayer is at 12:30 p.m. It begins with a sung alleluia and a Scripture is read in different languages. There are several songs, silence, a prayer by Brother Roger, then several more chants. Evening prayer is at 8:30 p.m. Again, we begin with an alleluia, Scripture, chants, silence, chants, a prayer by Brother Roger and closing songs.

I think what I love most about worship is the silence. We Protestants are fond of filling every moment of worship with noise. Church experts tell us that there cannot be any dead time in worship. People live in a world of intense and constant stimulation, which has to be replicated in worship or people will become bored. We demand something new and different every week to keep folks entertained.

Certainly, worship must be well planned and flow smoothly. However, most of us who plan worship neglect intentional periods of silence, including me. Having three 10-minute periods of silence every day is a pure gift for my spirit. Over the week I have come to relish that time as I completely turn off my mind, close my mouth and allow God to speak to me.

I often sit in front of an icon and meditate on the scene. It is a very mystical experience. Granted, at times I am plagued with distractions and cannot let go. At times, I cannot sit still. Other times, I insist on speaking to God rather than being quiet. I do know that when I return to active ministry, I want to regularly incorporate silence into worship.

I quickly adapt to the relaxed life of Taizé. I am awakened every morning at 8 a.m. by classical music, which permeates the building where I stay. After morning prayer, we eat a simple breakfast of bread, jam and coffee, tea or hot chocolate. I soon discover that at every meal we are given only a tray, a soup spoon and two plastic bowls. With so many people visiting Taizé, the food and method of serving has to be simple. It's amazing what you can do with a soup spoon. You can even butter bread and cut meat!

After breakfast we have a daily Bible study led by Brother Komo, who is from Africa. He speaks in both French and English, which seem to be the languages everyone can understand at least a little. Our Bible study this week is on the life of Joseph, which Brother Komo relates to an annual letter that Brother Roger writes for the worldwide Taizé community.

In the late morning we have free time, which I always use to go running. Taizé is located in a gorgeous part of Burgundy with rolling hills and lots of farms and villages dotting the landscape. It is pure pleasure every day, discovering new country roads on which to run. After midday prayer, we eat lunch. This week there are only about 60 visitors at Taizé, following 3,000 the week before. I'm glad I'm here during a slow week because I appreciate the peacefulness and serenity of the setting. Having 3,000 youth at Taizé would no doubt lend an air of excitement and spiritual energy, but I think I'm too old for that. I'd rather have quietness!

After lunch there is music practice for those who want to learn how to sing the songs of Taizé. In the mid-afternoon, the young people are put to work for a few hours, while we older folks have a group discussion time. Because there are so few older adults and the language barrier is a problem, we chose not to meet after the first day. This gives us time to go for long walks, take a nap or read. At 5:15 p.m., there is tea and cookies, with supper at 7:00 p.m., followed by evening prayer at 8:30 p.m. and then bed.

At evening prayer, a young man next to me falls asleep during the time of silence. He is kneeling with his head and elbows resting on the floor. All of a sudden, I hear quiet, gentle snoring. It's OK, I say to myself. If he needs to sleep, then he should sleep.

People fall asleep at First Church, too, most often during the sermon. Sometimes they apologize to me after the service. My reply is always the same, "If you need to sleep, by all means sleep. Actually, I'm glad you're relaxed enough in church that you can sleep. I'm not bothered, and neither is God."

* * *

One of the wonderful aspects of making a pilgrimage to Taizé is meeting Christians from all over the world. This week there are people from Germany, Austria, France, Holland, Liechtenstein, Poland, Korea, Scotland, Canada, Sweden, Mexico, Switzerland, the Philippines, Czechoslovakia and the Island of Réunion, near Madagascar.

Ullah and Eleanor are from Sweden. They met at a conference a few years ago and said they felt an immediate connection. They became soul mates, united by their common belief in God. When someone from our table wonders where her life is going, Eleanor looks her in the eye and says, "Follow your heart."

Pat and Nancy are Catholic sisters from Maryland who came to Taizé for two days while attending a conference in Paris. In a discussion about happiness, Nancy says, "I am happy when I am truly present to the moment, which means being truly present to God." Pat says, "I am happy when I let go of the facade and the defenses and can be who God calls me to be."

Yolanda is a young woman from Mexico. She has had a difficult life and says her family does not understand her spiritual struggles. She has found peace in Christ and is here for the second time.

Trudy is from Germany. She says it is easy to find God at Taizé, but we all have to go back to our normal lives, which is the real challenge. She tries to show her faith by her life, not mere words.

Jean is from the island of Réunion, near Africa. He says he comes to Taizé because this is a place of miracles. We come from so many different countries, yet we are one in Christ.

Isaac is a young man from Canada who is thinking of becoming a minister like his father. He is taking time off from his studies to nurture his spiritual life and seek direction from God.

Jacques is from Holland. He is a semi-retired engineer who lives in a Christian community in Eindhoven. They house refugees from all over the world and also have a home for youth. Jacques has been coming to Taizé for 40 years and has a vibrant faith.

Antje and Almut are from Germany. Antje, a physician who is a paraplegic because of a rock-climbing accident three years ago, is searching for meaning, direction and a new life. The things she wants to do she is no longer capable of doing and the things she is able to still do, she doesn't want to do. She says the most difficult part of life is that she can no longer be spontaneous. Going anywhere involves meticulously planning.

Almut, Antje's friend and a nurse, is seeking to increase her faith. She has a wonderfully warm spirit and invited me to come and visit her in Freiburg anytime.

I have been incredibly blessed by my friendship with Marcie. I met her less than a week ago but feel as if I've known her for years. It's amazing that we are the only Americans here for the entire week, yet we felt an immediate bond. I have had lots of time to myself, but I have thoroughly enjoyed my daily afternoon walks with Marcie. We have shared some of the deepest and most guarded parts of our lives, things few other people know about us. Who knows if we will ever see each other again? All I know is that God gave Marcie to me as a gift this week and I will always remember her gentle, loving spirit, the sparkle in her laugh and her search for herself and God. Thank you, Marcie.

* * *

My introspection has paralleled our nation's soul-searching after September 11. In our nation we cannot expect things to get back to normal too quickly. The horror is too great, the wounds too deep. It takes time. Rather than put it all behind us and get on with things, we should take time to think about why the terrorist attacks happened. It does not mean we accept blame, but we should try to understand why people would do this to us. What is our nation's role in the world? Have we exercised our power wisely? How do others perceive us? Do we need to change?

It's the same with me. Some will ask: Why do you need three months to look at yourself? It's because habits deeply ingrained over the years are difficult to recognize and acknowledge, let alone break. It's because, when I gradually drift away from God, it takes time to return. It's because, when my entire identity is tied up in my roles as pastor, mother and spouse, I need to let go of them entirely to receive a new identity as child of God. It's because, when I have lived a tightly controlled and controlling existence for so many years, I need time to allow the Spirit to master me. It's because, when I am addicted to work, sometimes the only way to change is to go cold turkey—absolutely no work for three months. It's because one does not discover new lands without consenting to lose sight of the shore for a very long time.

Just as with our nation, the introspection is painful. It involves peeling away layers of self-deception, denial and excuses. However, it is worth every second of agony as a new self and, I hope, a new nation will emerge: humbler, gentler, more tolerant and loving and less controlling and power-grabbing; a country characterized by acceptance, respect, reconciliation, and a greater willingness to be part of a world community.

* * *

At evening prayer on Friday at Taizé, the pilgrims remember the passion of Christ, his suffering and death for our world and us. Jesus had so much passion that he allowed himself to be passive: to be arrested, tortured, mocked, humiliated and put to death—all out of love for us. At the end of the service, the large icon of Jesus on the cross is placed on a table at the center of the church. As songs are sung, anyone who wishes can kneel, place their forehead on the cross and pray, allowing Jesus to wash away their sins and committing everything they have to Christ.

This morning, Brother Komo, who led our Bible study, reminds us of the symbolism of the cross. The vertical arm represents our relationship to God. The horizontal arm symbolizes community between people. The only way to reach God and other people is through Jesus, who hangs in the center of the cross. The only way to love is through the suffering love of Christ.

Before the service, I make a list of my failures, sins, shortcomings, character flaws, addictions and fears, all of which I want to release into the loving and welcoming arms of Jesus. Among them are pride, control, desire for attention, need for affirmation, not loving God first, keeping part of myself from God, addiction to work, lack of attention to my spirit and compulsive behaviors.

When I kneel at the cross and place my forehead on the top of the vertical arm, I feel the power of Christ surge through me. It is one of the most incredible experiences of my life. As great big tears drop onto the floor, I remember the tears that Jesus shed in the Garden of Gethsemane. He felt everything that I feel. Although he was innocent, he took it all upon himself. I pray:

Lord Jesus, I give myself to you. I want to begin a new life now. I empty myself completely. I give to you all of my fears and failures. I release them into your hands. Fill all of me with all of you. Let me be a pure expression of your love. All you want is for me to love you. I love you, God.

As I return to my seat, the tears continue to flow as we sing:

Your will is my song. I remember your name in the night.

Within our darkest night, you kindle the fire that never dies away.

Our darkness is never darkness in your sight: the deepest night is clear as the daylight.

Stay with me, remain here with me; watch and pray; watch and pray.

Into your hands, O Father, I commend my spirit.

Tonight is the culmination of the reflection, introspection and spiritual searching of my renewal leave. I am convinced that I would not have gotten as much out of this experience had I come in September. I don't think I would have been ready. Now I feel my spirit growing stronger as I grow in my love of God. Indeed, this has been a very self-focused time, but I needed it. And coming to Taizé, I have met many people from all over the world who have those same yearnings and are taking extended time away to nurture their spirit. Taizé is a pure gift to me.

* * *

Today, all those visiting from North America are invited to spend an hour with Brother Pedro to reflect on our experience at Taizé. There are four of us in addition to me: Marcie, two young Canadians and another American who is volunteering at Taizé for a year. We begin by talking about September 11. Brother Pedro says, "We felt a tremendous solidarity with Americans. The Paris newspaper *Le Monde* had this headline, 'We Are All New Yorkers,' echoing President Kennedy's famous statement in Berlin, '*Ich bin ein Berliner.*' It's a tragedy for the entire human family. We need to learn to act out of love, not fear. We should also take time for introspection and see how we might want or need to change because of what happened."

Dana, who was in Washington, D.C., on September 11, says, "How can I speak of peace at a time like this? Some of my friends get mad at me." We talk about the fact that every human is capable of great evil as well as great good and we are part of the evil against which we fight. Only from that place can peace come. We decide that many Americans simply cannot hear that we may be part of the problem and that our country has hidden motivations. As a nation, we tend to resist pain at all costs and are not very self-reflective. We also don't know how the rest of the world perceives us.

Isaac, a young man from Canada, reflects that simply by the way we live we take advantage of Third World countries. The food we eat, the clothes we buy and the gas we guzzle affects the rest of the world. At times, we are very irresponsible and wasteful in our lifestyles.

I comment that one of the gifts Taizé has given me is simplicity. Dana and Sandra, who are both taking a year off, talk about all the stuff they gave away before coming to Taizé. Possessions so often get in the way of our relationship with God.

Materialism is an evil just as insidious as the other isms. Living simply also means that we are closer to the margins of life and can take more risks. Brother Pedro comments that simplicity does not have to be austere. It can be beautiful and full of joy. He goes on to say that in the same way, our worship spaces are usually better off when we take things away to create a simpler space rather than add things.

The same principle works in the inner life, Isaac ventures. If we could only get rid of the "stuff" clogging our spirits, we would have more space for God. We conclude by talking about how we can live simple lives in the midst of affluence, at the same time realizing that we need to be sensitive to the needs of others around us. We must find a balance between personal and corporate spirituality.

It is a wonderful experience: a Taizé brother from Spain, an English and a French-speaking Canadian and Americans from Florida, California and Michigan gathering to reflect upon peace, reconciliation, simplicity and prayer.

Thank you, Jesus.

* * *

Tonight is another one of those moments when heaven and earth meet. After evening prayer, during which we all light candles in celebration of the resurrection, we are invited to meet and hear Brother Roger in the house where the brothers live. I have never seen anyone quite like Brother Roger. He fell and broke his wrist last week, so he is pretty fragile. About 80 of us, almost all young people under 30, cram into the brothers' dining room.

Fortunately, I am able to sit very near to Brother Roger. When he arrives, I notice right away that his face is overpowering. His face literally shines with the light and love of Christ. His smile, bright eyes and beautiful white hair are amazing. I truly see Christ in this man before he even opens his mouth. I can't help but think, *If only I could be like that. I want to have that kind of beautiful smile.*

Brother Roger's theology is summed up in one word: love. That's why hundreds of thousands of young people have been touched by Taizé over the last 61 years. The first comment he makes tonight is, "We Christians need to bear witness to the fact that human beings are not condemned. God looks on every human being with unending tenderness and profound compassion. God's love is for each human being, without exception."

He says that the imbalance between the accumulation of riches and poverty is perhaps the most critical question of our time. There is an urgency to help victims of poverty, and until that happens, there will not be peace in our world. He says, "Neither misfortune nor poverty come from God. God can only give love."

Brother Roger concludes by reminding us that Christ is united to each human being, without exception. Even if that person is not aware of it, Christ is united to them. To be united to all, we have to be willing to risk, to open new paths of communion. Too many of us, however, are trapped by fear. This causes us to withdraw, consolidate power and look inward. Most of all, we are called to communicate the mystery of hope, for God loves and understands each one of us. Our faith is only credible when it is lived. Only then can we communicate and pass on faith to others.

At the very end, Brother Roger says, "I want to see your faces." He sits in a chair, and one by one, as we walk by, his left hand grasps ours, and he looks right into our faces.

I think Brother Roger is a lot like Mother Teresa. He has never sought attention, yet he has inspired millions of lives. To greet him is truly a high privilege and a holy moment.

The Dark Night of the Soul

I never thought it would happen to me.

A night as black as black can be.

Gut-wrenching despair, hopelessness, depression, loneliness.

From where does my help come?

My help comes from the One who made heaven and earth.

My God, my God, why have you forsaken me?

Where am I? Why am I here? What are you doing to me?

Why am I feeling this way?

I am mired in quicksand.

Nothing I do can prevent me from sinking further into the muck.

Take my hand, precious Lord, lift me up. Lead me on. Renew my spirit.

Bless all those who feel this way every day and not once in a lifetime.

Bless all those who live in darkness through no fault of their own.

May I never forsake my brothers and sisters who suffer from illnesses of the mind, body and spirit, that prevents them from living in the light.

Do not let my darkness speak to me, God.

Stay with me.

Kindle a fire within my heart that will never go away.

Worship at Taize, France.

CHAPTER 11

Recess

AS I SUSPECT, when I return to Paris, I do not experience any of the feelings I had a week ago. Upon further reflection, I decide that I had a case of existential loneliness, a sort of melancholy of the spirit. I am convinced that at the core of every being is a sense of utter aloneness. We recognize our insignificance and nothingness in the grand scheme of the world and the finiteness of our life. We realize that even though we may have family and friends surrounding us, in the end the journey through life is ours alone.

I often sense this when I am ministering to people who are dying. Dying is a very lonely experience because no one can walk the path with us. We may have loved ones who will do anything for us, but they cannot die for us. As the dying process progresses toward its conclusion, I observe people withdrawing from their surroundings. They already have one foot in heaven. Their focus is beginning to move from this life to the life to come. That gradual withdrawal is necessary and also helpful because it is easier for loved ones to let go.

I have always liked St. Augustine's words, "Our hearts are made for you, O Lord, and they will not rest until they rest in you." We are, indeed, made for God. That's what it means to be created in the image of God. We have a void in us that only God can fill. That restlessness, that longing for meaning, that yearning for God finds fulfillment when we welcome Jesus Christ into our life. It seems to me, however, that some sense of existential loneliness will persist until we are finally reunited with God at the time of death.

Most of the time we are not aware of our loneliness. We are very good at covering it up with distractions, noise and busyness—anything to prevent us from having to face our true selves. Joyce Rupp writes in her book *Praying Our Goodbyes* that it is only when we embrace the "absolute truth" of our aloneness that we realize we are not truly alone. In fact, we break through to a higher level of awareness of our bonding with God and others. This, then, is the source of spiritual growth.

Last Saturday, I came face to face with my utter aloneness and it was terrifying. Now I have a better understanding that my aloneness is part of being human. When I recognize that loneliness, I am empowered to love without holding on, to be without control and to touch at the deepest levels of spirit as I let go.

* * *

I arrive at my hotel in the early afternoon. It's in a great location along the West Bank and within walking distance of many sights in Paris. In my exploration, I first stop at Notre Dame Cathedral, where I catch the tail end of a most impressive worship service celebrating Armistice Day. I wish I could have been there the whole time because the British are leading the service in English. For the postlude, the organist plays Sir Edward Elgar's "Pomp and Circumstance," which brings on the tears. I don't think I have ever heard an organ so powerful. The reverberation rolls around the cathedral for many seconds.

I return later in the afternoon for an organ recital, which is wonderful. I say special prayers during the concert for my parents, thanking them for giving me a love of music. If they hadn't made music an important part of their life, I probably would not have either. My father has sung in church choirs for 60 years, virtually all his life, and both Mom and Dad enjoy classical music and attend frequent concerts. If it hadn't been for them, I would not be sitting in Notre Dame today.

Despite Notre Dame's immensity, it feels safe. It feels warm. I sense that the spirit of God is here giving off light and ministering to each one of the thousands of people who pass through every day.

* * *

It is great to see Gary. We are now both officially at recess. He is in good spirits but utterly exhausted from the overnight flight and three months of stressful ministry. On the bus from the airport into Paris Gary fills me in on what has been happening at the church and how good attendance has been—incredible, in fact. The stewardship campaign is going well, music and worship have been outstanding and there is a sweet spirit. I jokingly tell Gary that since I'm not needed any more, I don't have to come back. I actually mean it. I have been able to detach enough, especially after being in Taizé, that I don't need to be a pastor anymore to fulfill my own needs. I have God, and that is enough.

This afternoon I read a section of Carlo Caretto's *The God Who Comes*, where he says that when we find and experience God in the depths of our being and live in the "fire of his Trinity and the bliss of his Unity"—then we realize that God alone is enough. Now I understand.

* * *

On Gary's first full day in Paris, we do a lot of walking. We walk to the top of the Arc de Triomphe, visit Sainte-Chapelle and Notre Dame and go through the museum on the history of Paris.

We also go to a chocolate shop and buy about $100 worth of chocolate, including a $50 assortment for our staff. When the cashier tallies up the bill, it only comes out to $38. I question her at the time, and she says it is correct. As we are eating lunch, we are still uneasy about the transaction. Gary suggests perhaps I was confusing francs with euros and I reply that there is no way we could have purchased all that chocolate from such a fine shop for only $38. Gary asks me to take out the receipt. I look it over carefully and discover that the clerk simply forgot to add in the $50 box of chocolate.

What should we do? It is clear we have to go back, for we were terribly undercharged. The original clerk is not there, but the manager is. She is most happy to see us and we straighten it out. We could have very well gone on our way, pocketing the extra $50. It would have been easy, but it was not right.

When we were back home, we told the story to our children, then posed the question, "What would you have done?" One of them quickly said we were crazy to go back. Then we asked, "What if you were that clerk and when your mistake was discovered they took $50 out of your next paycheck?" We face these questions every day in one form or another, don't we? I am grateful that I am a Christian. It gives me a good frame of reference to discern what is ethical and right.

* * *

Today we visit the National Museum of the Middle Ages (Musée de Cluny) and the Louvre. It has been 25 years since I have wandered through museums. I never felt I had time before, so it is nice to leisurely stroll through the galleries.

We are particularly interested in the Lady with the Unicorn tapestries in the Museum of the Middle Ages. Talitha has been fascinated with unicorns since she was little and has an extensive collection. Also, one of the tapestries shows the lady playing an organ.

The unicorn has long been a Christ figure. In the early centuries of Christianity, in the city of Alexandria, a book was published which became known as the *Physiologus*. The book contained descriptions of every beast known to humankind and allegories connecting them to their place in creation. Although considered heretical by official Christendom, this book had great influence over the next thousand years.

According to the *Physiologus*, the unicorn horn signifies the unity of Christ and Father God. The inability of the hunter alone to capture the unicorn is a reminder that the will of the Messiah is not subject to any earthly authority. Also, the unicorn's small stature is a sign of Christ's humility. Because of Talitha, unicorns will always have a special place in my heart.

The Louvre is an amazing place. It's so big that we hardly know where to start. There is a sense in which all art is religious art, as it conveys the deepest longings of the artist. However, the art with which I often identify revolves around specific biblical stories or theological concepts.

We are only able to have a whirlwind tour of the Louvre, and I wish for more time to meditate on individual paintings. What I come away with is pure awe that God has given people gifts to paint, draw, weave and sculpt. Almost everything I see occasions a "Wow!" and the thought, "How can people do that?" The power of one. These museums have awakened in me a desire to learn more about art and history. Oh, that I had the time. Where will I get the time?

* * *

I've started thinking about returning to active ministry. I have two weeks left and know that when I arrive home on Sunday, much of the last 10 days will be spent preparing for Advent. I will also have to do some intentional work on setting priorities and deciding how my life is going to be structured. There won't be nearly the time I've had for reading, prayer and meditation, but I will have to carve out some space.

Most of all, I need to learn how—at all times and in every moment of the day—to pay attention to God and be a vehicle for God's love. In his book, *Reaching Out*, Henri Nouwen talks about a priest who canceled his subscription to *The New York Times* because he felt the constant stories about violence, crime and misuse of power prevented him from being able to meditate and pray.

Nouwen explains this as a sad story because it implies that the only way we can live in the world is to deny it and that the only way to live the spiritual life is to surround ourselves by an "artificial, self-induced quietude." For Nouwen, a genuine spiritual life does the opposite. It makes us more alert to the world around us and frees us to gather up everything that happens as part of all that is. It also invites both contemplation and bold response. "Brothers and sisters, do not be weary in doing what is right." (2 Thessalonians 3:13) By being alert and aware of the world around me but not becoming a quivering mass of availability, I hope that, moving forward, I will not weary in doing what is right.

* * *

We have a wonderful lunch today after visiting the Musée d'Orsay. It is one of the few times in my life that I order veal, which is so very tender. And the apple pie—unbelievable! The food in Paris has been exquisite. Never before have I experienced food prepared so well and presented so beautifully. Even though food has never been that important to me, eating in Paris in such intimate, elegantly appointed restaurants has been a spiritually satisfying as well as a physically satisfying experience.

Our bountiful lunch gives us the energy to walk to the Eiffel Tower on a very cold day. While waiting in line we meet an American woman named Anna. Anna is traveling by herself from England to Paris for a few days, then back to London and home to Florida. When we reach the front of the line, Anna realizes that they do not take credit cards and she has virtually no French money. We give her the $11 admission fee and go up to the top together. It is really fun and really cold, especially when I convince Gary to walk partway back down. On the way we see an incredible sunset.

* * *

She is the saddest-looking person I have ever seen. Gary and I sit across from her in the subway. Her eyes are moist. She dabs at them every so often with a tissue. She is doing everything she can to remain composed. Next to her is a young boy around 8 years old. Her skin is white. His skin is black. The boy obviously knows something is wrong. His hands clutch her left arm, their heads lean against each other. Both fear and love are in his eyes. Something terrible has happened. She is weeping and he doesn't know what to do except simply be there for her. They don't say a word to each other during the time we ride together. Then they leave, her feet dragging, head bowed, the little boy trying to hold her up. I send continual prayers her way, trusting that God will care for her.

* * *

It is our last day in France. We decide not to push it too much because we want to do a little shopping. We discover a wonderful gourmet food store, Fauchon, which is right next to the Madeleine Church. After a while, all churches look the same, but this church seems different because it is right in the middle of a busy shopping square. The square is jammed with Saturday shoppers, but inside the church it is quiet and peaceful.

I have the sense that churches in France, and perhaps Europe in general, are more of a sanctuary than they are in the United States. After all, the very word "sanctuary," which refers to the most sacred part of a religious building, where the altar is located, also means a place of refuge or protection. In times past, people fleeing the authorities sought out churches because they knew they would be safe. No one could capture them or harm them as long as they were inside the church.

So today a sanctuary is a refuge where people can come to sit, meditate and pray. It's a place where they can get away from the noise and stress of life outside in order to rest and draw close to God. In every church we visited in Paris, numerous people were sitting and praying. Why is it, then, that many of our churches in the United States are locked, even during the day? How can a church be a sanctuary if it is not accessible to the people? First Church is open from 6:30 a.m. to 9:00 p.m. and I trust that we will never even consider locking the doors.

* * *

It is my last run along the Seine. A young Japanese couple already out sightseeing is looking for someone to take their picture. They eagerly motion for me to help them. It is obvious they are madly in love with each other, and they deeply appreciate that I stop to help them. We never exchange a word, but they give me the loveliest smiles you could imagine.

At the end of my run, I go into Notre Dame one last time. A mass is taking place at the front of the church, so I kneel along a side aisle to say prayers of thanksgiving to God. In this holy place, I ask God to help me lay aside all of the hassles and distractions that will hit me when I get home. I pray that I will focus solely on loving God and emptying myself so that the Spirit can master me and mold me into God's servant. The goal? That I might glorify God in everything I do. I pray that I will continually pay attention and see God everywhere I go.

We arrive home safe and sound.

A Unicorn Faith

Unicorn tapestries, unicorn pillows, unicorn sweaters;

Unicorn sculptures, unicorn posters; unicorn earrings;

Unicorn faith.

Unable to be captured by the hunter;

Symbol of the humility, purity and healing powers of Christ.

Unicorn mystery.

Unicorn drawings on placemats, napkins, and notebooks;

Container of the hopes and dreams of a little girl;

Unicorn music boxes, unicorn children's books, unicorn DVDs;

Unicorn trust.

A little girl smitten with visions of unicorns,

Even seeing one outside a department store in Grand Rapids;

Believing the horn has magical powers;

Symbol of the unity of Jesus and God.

O, for a unicorn faith of a little girl;

A faith that believes in miracles;

A faith convinced that God is the Lord of creation,

Jesus is the Savior of the world,

And people are at heart good and noble and pure.

Unicorn hope.

At the top of Notre Dame.

CHAPTER 12

Preparation

WHILE JOGGING TODAY back in Grand Rapids I run into someone from the church, so I stop and chat with him for a while. A church member brings dinner to the house tonight, and I decide I cannot hide in my bedroom, so I meet her at the door and have a wonderful conversation. Grand Rapids is not a huge city, so I know that in the course of the next 10 days I simply will not be able to avoid people. What I have to do is remain somewhat detached at the same time as I gradually re-enter life as a pastor.

In Richard Foster and Emilie Griffin's book, *Spiritual Classics*, they include a unique translation by Bill Griffin of a portion of Thomas a Kempis' *The Imitation of Christ*. Although Kempis was writing in Latin 650 years ago from a monastic point of view, his emphasis upon the inner life of solitude and warning against busyness and preoccupation with social obligations speaks deeply to my heart. He says that if we want to cultivate our interior life, we must spend time with Jesus, for it is in solitude that our soul makes progress, the Scriptures are opened and we weep with devotion.

Thomas posits two courses of action. "Better, to lie still in one's cubicle and worry about one's spiritual welfare. Worse, to roam the streets a wonder-worker for others to the neglect of one's own spiritual life." That last sentence describes the danger of my life—roaming the streets of Grand Rapids, feeling I have to be a wonder-worker for others while neglecting my own inner life. I vow to change that.

* * *

I believe I will be ready by the end of next week to go back to work. I am already doing a lot of preparation at home, so it will not be so much of a shock. Gary and I are discussing plans for Advent, Christmas and the new year and I find that I am now able to enter into those conversations willingly.

I have discovered, however, that I have little interest and patience for the arguments that arise over petty issues. How true it is that the issues that elicit the most dissension in churches are incredibly stupid when looked at from the outside. For example, the current dispute is over which brand of coffee the church should use. After eight years of buying store-bought coffee, suddenly two different groups are lobbying for a change. How we pastors get in the middle of such decisions is beyond me. Suffice it to say, after three months of working on my spiritual life, I've decided not to get worked up over coffee. Besides, I don't even drink coffee!

Another dispute has arisen over the flags. When we remodeled the sanctuary a few years ago, we removed the American and Christian flags from the front of the sanctuary. We intended to place them in the narthex next to the plaques honoring First Church members who fought in our 20th century wars. The plaques needed to be repaired, however, and we hadn't gotten to it because of all the other renovation around the church. Therefore, the flags were not out on September 11. Of course, the flags soon appeared in the narthex, which was fine with Gary and me. We did not want them to re-enter the sanctuary, however, because the Christian church transcends any national or political identity.

Then there's the poinsettia problem. For years we'd purchased poinsettias from a local florist, with church members giving them in memory of or in honor of a loved one. They would decorate the sanctuary during December and then be taken home after the Christmas Eve services. Last year a group of students at our partner elementary school wanted to sell poinsettias as a fundraiser. We thought that was a great idea and gave people two options: buy from the school kids or from the florist. This year we have attempted to make things easier by only selling poinsettias through the school, but it has been extremely complicated getting it all worked out.

I don't mean to minimize any of these concerns, but they are admittedly small in the grand scheme of the church. I am very glad that First Church does not usually become obsessed with little things. We try very hard to address quickly and openly each issue as it arises. Many times it is not Gary and me but other staff who put out the fires. Other times we all have to get our heads together and come up with a solution. By cultivating spiritual maturity and focusing on the big picture, we have avoided succumbing to the tyranny of the petty.

* * *

At 11:15 a.m. I realize that I had a hair appointment at 11 a.m. My hair stylist, who is a member of the church, is very gracious and takes me anyway. She decides that if I can miss an appointment, I am now truly relaxed.

Every day it seems as if I am running into several members of the church. I'm amazed that it feels OK. I am able to talk with them and find out how they are doing without bringing up the church. I am most grateful for their sensitivity.

I have been reading about solitude and silence this week. Richard Foster writes that silence opens the door to the universe where God is in charge, not us, and where God's love floods our spirit. And John Main, in his book *Moments of Christ: The Path of Meditation*, says that using words is essential for humans, yet in order for those words to have power we have to practice silence.

I have always been a quiet person, but after this renewal leave, I am more convinced than ever of the need for silence and solitude. I have also made a commitment to try to think before I speak. As a pastor, I easily fall victim to believing that people look to me for answers, and I am more than happy to oblige them. Many times I speak without saying anything significant. I venture an opinion without knowing all the facts. I use words to control others or to project a positive image of myself. I vow to remember that God is in charge of this world. I am not.

After weeks spent in solitude, I realize that everyone can carry on nicely without me, that I am not indispensable, that it's even OK to be forgotten. Only by leaving the church completely and for a long time could I gain a proper perspective on my true role as a pastor. Solitude has given me the space to see how arrogant, presumptuous and manipulative I often am in my conversations.

Main summarizes why I took this leave. He says that unless you and I can rediscover the spiritual aspect of our existence, we can easily lose our grip on life altogether. I really did feel as if I was losing my grip on life. Now I know that keeping close to God by nurturing my spiritual life is what will keep me on track.

* * *

Garth came home late last night, and Sarah just came home 10 minutes ago. Right now all three children are upstairs talking and laughing, and I am in heaven. I love my children so much and am very grateful that they are good friends. It wasn't that way for a number of years when Sarah was struggling and our whole family was in turmoil. Now that our children are older and are in different schools, I think it is easier for them to accept each other. In fact, a few weeks ago Sarah went to Ann Arbor to visit Garth on a Saturday, something I never dreamed would happen a few years ago. We will all be together for Thanksgiving.

Thank you, God, for my family.

* * *

Thanksgiving Day! Thanksgiving always comes at a good time for me. Two days off after a very busy fall at the church provides an opportunity to do a little Christmas shopping and a chance to prepare myself mentally and physically for December and Advent, my least favorite time of the year.

I've been amazed at how calm I have been feeling. Certainly, much of that is due to the fact that I am not yet officially back to work. I do not fall into bed at night bone-weary, aching all over from one day after another of frenetic activity. I am much more physically rested, but I also feel an inner peace that was not there before. I have discovered that it may not be as easy as I think to incorporate devotional time into my daily life. Not only do things seem to come up constantly to disturb that time, but I also have to learn how to be firm with others about the sacredness of that time.

We have a very nice Thanksgiving dinner with the five of us. I was going to say "nice quiet Thanksgiving dinner," but with three teenagers, our house is never quiet. There is nonstop banter, joking, reminiscing and dreaming. I love it! Rarely are we able to convince all three children to do something with us, but in the late afternoon, we all go to see the IMAX movie *Everest*. Amazingly, everyone likes it.

In the evenings, all of the children go out with their friends and come home far after I've gone to bed. When Sarah was in high school, Gary and I felt we had to wait up until she came home—and for good reason! We had many a sleepless night, and more than once we were awakened in the middle of the night by phone calls. It's taken me a long time to let go of that uneasy feeling of going to bed before I know our children are all safe. I've had to do it, however, because of my own sanity. I simply have to trust that God will take care of them.

I am truly thankful for all of God's blessings, foremost among them my family. I can't believe Gary and I have three beautiful children who are so very different than we are. They are certainly unique individuals and I can't wait to see what God does with their lives.

* * *

Earlier in my leave, I vowed to review my personal mission statement in light of my experiences over the past three months. My statement read, **"My mission is to serve God and make a positive difference in the world by taking care of myself and my family, ministering in my local church and working to bring in the kingdom for all of God's children."**

As I spend time today meditating on my mission, I feel that the priorities are in the right order: God, self, family, local church and world. What I notice is that the statement is all action: I vow to serve, make a difference, take care, minister and work. Missing is any element of being, waiting, loving, obedience. One of my greatest learnings has been that my only calling is to love God. When I am able to be quiet and passive—when I set aside my own agenda for ministry—then God can work through me.

In his spiritual classic, *A Testament of Devotion*, first published in 1941, Thomas Kelly talks about gateways into holy obedience. Whereas some people meet God through a profound mystical experience, others pursue obedience through active struggle, like Jacob wrestling with the angel until the morning dawns. In this way our will "must be subjected bit by bit, piecemeal and progressively, to the divine Will."

I am afraid the active way describes me. For me, obedience involves struggle with my ego, my needs and my desire to "do it myself." All is not lost, however, for Kelly goes on to say that arrival at holy obedience involves nothing more than simply beginning. We begin where we are, and God takes it from there. Kelly writes that rather than grit our teeth and determine to follow God's will, we ought to relax, unclench our fists and submit ourselves to God. He says, "Learn to live in the passive voice—a hard saying for Americans—and let life be willed through you."

Here is my revised personal mission statement:

"My mission is to love God and allow God to work through me to make a positive difference in the world. I vow to take care of myself and my family, serve those in my local church and work to bring in the kingdom for all of God's children."

Living in the Passive Voice

Who will I be when life goes back to normal?

What will normal be?

How will I act when the rat race of the everyday threatens to run amuck again?

Will I be a quivering mass of availability or a centered, serene disciple of Jesus?

Will I roam the streets as a wannabe wonder-worker, neglecting my spiritual life;

Or can I learn how to say no?

The afterglow of this leave will wear off. Then what?

I guess I meet God in the wrestling, just like Jacob.

I guess I unclench my fists.

I guess I let go so that the Holy Spirit can master me.

I guess I learn to live in the passive voice,

Inviting God's intentions to be willed through me.

My mission: to love God and allow God to work through me to make a difference in the world.

It's not about me anymore.

And that is certainly not normal.

At least for me.

A new normal?
What's holding me back?

As we celebrate the God
who became incarnate
and lived among us,
may we offer our lives
in joyful response.

Gary & Laurie,
Sarah, Garth & Talitha Haller

Family Christmas picture 2001.

CHAPTER 13

Re-Entry

DURING THIS LAST week, I am working on changes that I need to make in my life. I told Gary the other day that this leave has been the best thing that has ever happened to me. Notice, though, I didn't say my leave was the best thing I have ever done. However I have changed is due to my allowing God to work through me.

I vow to intentionally seek out times of worship when I have no leadership responsibilities. Worship has been so fulfilling on my leave. I have been free to let my spirit roam, soar and enter into communion with God. When I am leading a service, it's almost impossible to worship because I am preoccupied with so many other details. My role as a pastor has left me unable to be sustained and nourished by practices that are normative for other Christians.

I vow to set aside at least half an hour a day for Bible and spiritual reading, meditation, prayer and journal keeping. I have discovered that spiritual disciplines keep me open to the God who wants nothing more than to reside in my heart. For years, Bible-reading and prayer have been reduced to tools of the trade and have not always been personally fulfilling. I talk about spiritual matters so much that I lose a sense of the spirituality in my own life. The Bible needs to become more than sermon material but a way to personally encounter God.

I vow to find a spiritual guide with whom I will meet regularly. It is important to have someone with whom I can share and to whom I can be accountable for my spiritual life.

I vow to take more time for study and solitude. I also will try to take one retreat day a month. Doing this will keep me alive spiritually so that other pastoral work will benefit rather than suffer.

I vow to become more detached from my work so that I can better serve my parishioners. Three months ago I would have thought exactly the opposite: The more attached I am to my people, the better I can serve them. Now I know that much of what I have done in ministry has been governed by my own needs rather than the needs of others. Being a "quivering mass of availability" only frazzles my nerves, runs me ragged and burns me out.

I vow to become a better listener. People are more willing to confide in others when they sense a readiness and ability to listen carefully and compassionately. My habit of continually being distracted takes away from focusing completely on the person with whom I am talking.

I vow to give up control and allow the Spirit to master me.

I vow to start a Taizé service at First Church. I believe there is a need for more spiritual growth opportunities at First Church and will work to identify, train and empower people in that area.

I vow to find more opportunities to sing and play the organ. I will attend more concerts and plays.

I vow to get enough rest so that I am not continually exhausted.

* * *

I am gradually beginning the process of re-entry into life as usual. This morning I go to my twice-weekly exercise class at the health club for the first time in three months. I've been part of this conditioning class for four and a half years and have come to love my fellow runners. This is the only group of people outside church friends with whom I am even somewhat close. The rest of my life revolves totally around the church. These friends don't care what I do or who I am. Most of them only know my first name. We are united by our love of running. By seeing each other twice a week, however, we do get to know each other more than superficially. I feel a sense of community there. My friends were not expecting me to return until next week, so I surprise them. I discover that I have kept in shape pretty well over the past three months and could keep up just fine.

This morning I have to give the church phone number to someone and discover I have forgotten it. I forgot it! Is that what three months away does to people?

We receive a Christmas card today from a woman whose name I do not recognize in the least. It is so strange. I think, how many folks are there going to be at church this Sunday whom I will not know? People have already joined the church this fall whom I have never met.

I am trying to work on the worship service for this Sunday and I hardly knew where to begin. I had to ask Gary, how are we doing worship now?

This afternoon I run into a church member in the grocery store. She greets me with a big smile and we hug. We're going to have lots of hugs on Sunday, of that I am sure. I believe in hugs. I hug everyone who comes through the line after church unless people offer their hand instead.

Some of my male colleagues, in particular, don't hug. They say it's too dangerous because people can misinterpret their intention. I suppose they are right, but I am willing to take the risk. A good hug conveys warmth, love and caring in a way that a handshake never will. It's funny, but no one in my exercise class gave me a hug this morning except for one young woman who is a preacher's kid. I don't think the others in my class are church folks. Makes a difference, I think.

* * *

The Harry Potter movie came out a few weeks ago, and Talitha has already seen it twice. Because of the concern of conservative Christians around the use of magic, sorcery and witchcraft in the book and movie, I decide it's time to read the book myself. Actually, it's quite entertaining. I take a more casual approach to books like *Harry Potter and the Sorcerer's Stone*. I loved fantasy as a child and read Tolkien's *The Hobbit* and *The Lord of the Rings* trilogy when I was in seventh grade. I think adults get more bent out of shape than children do about the magic aspect of the book and overlook the important themes like friendship, trust, loyalty and courage.

My favorite part of the book is when Harry found the Mirror of Erised. When he looked into the mirror, he saw his mother and father smiling at him. His parents were killed when he was a baby and Harry dearly missed having a normal family. When his friend Ron looked in the Mirror of Erised, he saw himself as captain of the Quidditch team, holding both the house cup and the Quidditch cup. The Mirror of Erised reflected their most cherished dreams.

Harry didn't understand what the mirror was all about until headmaster Albus Dumbledore explained that the happiest man on earth uses the Mirror of Erised like a normal mirror because he can see himself exactly as he is. The mirror shows us "nothing more or less than the deepest, most desperate desire of our hearts. ... It does not do to dwell on dreams and forget to live, remember that."

Quite a profound thought for a children's book, but one that spoke directly to me. Some people live in the past. They yearn for what can never be. They feel they can only be happy by recreating what was. Others live in the future. They dream unrealistically about what probably never will be. They feel they will only be happy if life is different than it is. The key to happiness is learning to live fully in the present and be satisfied with who we are.

In the past three months I have learned to enjoy each day for the gift that it is. I have to take time now to do what I love because tomorrow may never come. That will mean a change of priorities and attitude. I hope I can do it.

* * *

Today I invite three close friends from the church to go out for lunch. I have not seen them for three months, but we have had occasional email contact. I am very nervous about seeing them again. It's funny. I have prayed for them by name every day for three months, yet when I actually see them face-to-face, it is pure joy—like seeing the face of God. All I can do is peer intently into their eyes and smile. They look great!

One reason I want to get together is because I need to ease back into working and seeing familiar faces again. Having lunch with three friends is certainly less overwhelming than an entire congregation, whom I will see on Sunday. At first, I feel a bit awkward. So much has happened in the past three months in their lives and in mine—where to begin? We all have school-age children, so we start with them, then work our way into sharing how our spirits have been.

I have difficulty articulating what I have experienced over the past three months. I really don't know how to put into words what is in my heart. I fumble around, trying to describe the process of detachment and how I have come to the point where I do not need to go back to work. I have a new identity now that is not tied to my role as pastor. They know me well, so they understand. I explain my obsession with work and ask if they will agree to help me in the process of becoming a different kind of pastor.

Of course, they all say yes. These three women are spiritually wise, and I count it a privilege to call them friends. I am also confident that they will call me to task when they see me working too hard or becoming too frazzled or losing my focus.

* * *

As I am showering this morning, I experience a revelation. I am happy. I am truly happy! In the countless times a friend has asked me over the past six years, "Are you happy?" I don't think I have ever answered yes. I've rationalized my unhappiness by saying that joy is more important than happiness, and I haven't lost my joy. I was too afraid to ask myself, however, why I wasn't happy.

Now I know. For many years I lived with a certain restlessness. I was not content with my life but didn't think I could do anything about it. I was buffeted about by the demands of a busy church and an active family and said I was doing the best I could. I was enslaved to work and tied to my identity as a pastor. I was disconnected with the source of my life. As a realist, I figured I'd just have to accept the way it is.

The discontent only intensified, however, until I decided to take this renewal leave. That prompted me to look critically at my life and unmask the poverty of my spirit. Henri Nouwen has a good image in *Making All Things New* where he compares our overcrowded lives with an over-packed suitcase bursting at the seams. More than once in my life, I've had to sit on my suitcase to get it closed. And more than once, I've had to tape my suitcase all over so it didn't pop open.

In the same way, my life has been filled with everything but God. When I reached the point where I was ashamed of all the clutter, rather than clean out the suitcase I simply wrapped it with more tape. In the last three months, I finally opened the suitcase to let out 20-years'-worth of accumulation and began making a place for God.

The reason I have been unhappy is that I have not been centered in God. The things I did and the affirmation I received became more important than God. Now I have begun the process of allowing the Spirit to recreate me into one who is filled with peace. I was not searching for happiness, but in the process of learning how to love God and allow myself to be mastered by the Spirit, I suddenly discovered happiness staring me in the face.

I told my friends yesterday that I feel more centered and calm than I have in 25 years. Most people will not observe that by simply looking at me. I am the same on the outside. Inside, however, I have been changed and transformed. It's not to say I won't be busy come next Monday. Being a pastor in a large church always will be demanding. And I don't think God necessarily wants me to be less busy. God only wants me to realign my priorities. God wants to be the center of my attention. When love of God comes before anything else, I am convinced that I will be able to stay centered and grounded.

Staying rooted in God will mean hard work and determination on my part, for there are many forces that will pull me back into chaos if I am not careful. Creating inner space to listen to God can only happen by deliberately and intentionally engaging in spiritual disciplines. I must take time every day to give God my undivided attention.

So ... I am happy. I am filled with the light of God's love. I am ready to go back into ministry with enthusiasm and zeal.

* * *

The theologian Paul Tillich once said, "Religion is first an open hand to receive a gift, and second, an active hand to distribute gifts. What we are is God's gift to us, what we become is our gift to God." God has given me so many gifts over the past three months. I can scarcely believe it. My experience has been far more than I could have ever dreamed or imagined. What I become because of my renewal leave is my gift to God.

I am still committed to doing. I will always be an activist. A few years ago I read the book *Having Our Say*. It's a fascinating account of two African-American professional women, Sadie and Bessie Delaney, and the changes they saw over the past century. Sadie, a high school teacher, and Bessie, a dentist, both lived to be well over 100 years old. They never married because married women at the time were not allowed to continue in their careers.

Sadie and Bessie had a secure family upbringing, their father becoming the first black Episcopal bishop in America. They wrote about their childhood that the Delaney family creed centered on improving oneself through education, service and ethical living along with a strong belief in God. The family motto was, "Your job is to help somebody." According to Sadie and Bessie, this code applied to anyone who needed help regardless of color. They were brought up to help people, not to receive any reward or so that people would applaud them. They did it because of the example set by Jesus and by their parents.

I believe my calling is to help other people—especially to empower them to connect to God through Jesus Christ and facilitate transformation. I am committed to using every gift I have been given to that end. I have always liked this statement of Edmund Burke, "Nobody makes a greater mistake than he who did nothing because he could only do a little."

I also know, however, that I have to learn how to *be* as well as *do*. Over the past three months, I have come to see that I am not as important as I used to think. I am not as indispensable as I had hoped to be. (Gary did just fine without me!) Not every task I think I need to do is pressing, nor must it be done by me. My focus now has to turn to listening rather than always speaking; reflecting rather than always acting; being rather than always doing; and attending to God rather than to the urgent, the necessary or the desirable.

O God, help me to expect nothing from myself and everything from you.

* * *

At 5:29 p.m. Friday evening, I put on panty hose and a dress for the first time in three months for a wedding rehearsal. I guess that means I am back to work. When I left in September, our sanctuary was still being repainted and the scaffolding was up. Walking into the finished sanctuary last night took my breath away. It was absolutely stunning. I have been in numerous churches over the past three months, but none were as gorgeous as ours. I guess I am biased.

The rehearsal is uneventful except for a conversation with the aunt of the bride, whose husband is a minister in California. The bride, groom and I had been discussing which version of the Lord's Prayer to use in the wedding: "debts," "trespasses," or "sins." At First Church we always use "sins" because it is easier for people to understand.

The aunt comments after the rehearsal, "Aren't you going to say 'Our Creator, who art in heaven' instead of 'Our Father, who art in heaven?' That's what we say every Sunday in Berkeley, and nobody blinks an eye."

I reply, "I have to admit that I've never heard the Lord's Prayer said that way. I often use 'Creator, Redeemer and Sustainer' instead of the traditional Trinitarian formula, 'Father, Son and Holy Spirit,' but I'm not sure our church would be ready to change the beginning of the Lord's Prayer to 'Our Creator, who art in heaven.' Remember, this is Grand Rapids, Michigan, not Berkeley, California." We both laugh.

As the groomsmen and I are waiting for the wedding service to begin, the three men decide to each bet a dollar on when the groom would start crying. One said it would be as the bride walked down the aisle, another said it would be during the groom's declaration of intent, and the third said it would be during the vows. They ask me to be the judge. It is during the sermon that the groom's eyes welled up. Because none of the men guessed correctly, I declare myself the winner and earn three dollars for the church.

I come home from the wedding believing that I am ready to be back in ministry. I make my first church-related phone calls, tying up some loose ends for Sunday morning worship. I've even lost the anxiety that I was feeling for the past week and a half. I believe that by working on the priorities I have set for myself, I am providing a network of support and account-ability that will keep me on track.

* * *

I didn't sleep well last night. I never do on Saturdays. I am too keyed up for Sunday morning. I awaken at 5:15 a.m., a half-hour earlier than I had planned. My pre-preaching diar-rhea comes back after a three-month hiatus. I go for my early morning run. I make myself eat some cereal and am off to the church. It is easier than I expected. It is always easier when I remember that people love me for who I am and not how well I "perform." It seems so natural to be back. There are hundreds of hugs, which is very special for me. It almost seems as if I was never gone—as if the last three months were a dream.

There are noticeable changes in many congregation mem-bers, however. Some have aged more than would be normal for three months. Children have grown taller. Babies were born. Some women are now pregnant. Some people have casts, some now use canes, and others have lost hair due to chemo-therapy. Some have lost family members to death. At least five men lost their jobs while I was gone.

How wonderful to celebrate communion on my first Sun-day back. What could give me more joy than looking people in the eye and saying, "Joe, this is the body of Christ given for you. Jane, this is the blood of Christ given for you." I realize how much I am loved and how much I love my congregation.

* * *

My first official day back at the office. I write the following article for our weekly newsletter:

> *I am thrilled to be back! I don't even know how to tell you what it has meant to have had this time away. Perhaps I can begin by sharing some of what I have learned about myself in the process of losing sight of the shore for a very long time.*

Central to effective ministry is the quality of my relationship with God. Keeping my soul alive is the most important activity in which I can engage as a pastor. This has been a primary learning for me. Growing in my personal faith is not an option or something to which I can tend when everything else is done. It is an essential part of my calling.

My search for God over the past three months has been filled with joy and pain, hope and despair, light and darkness. I learned that all God desires is that I love God. That meant a complete emptying of self. I've had to let go of many things I have tried to control in the past. I had to identify and face my failures, inadequacies, fears and false sense of importance.

I experimented with different spiritual disciplines. Because I was free of pastoral responsibilities, Scripture, spiritual reading, meditation and prayer were no longer simply sermon material or tools of the trade but became intensely fulfilling.

I had no idea how liberating it would be not to have 14 hours of every day packed with meetings and appointments. Not being preoccupied with lesser realities, I was able to sense Divine Reality in a new way. I spent a lot of time outside, reconnecting with God and nature, paying attention to everything around me. I learned how to fly fish, played some golf, took long walks along the beach and went to concerts, recitals and plays. Writing became a way to express the longings of my heart.

Disengaging from First Church proved to be the greatest challenge of my time away. Sundays were very difficult; as I imagined everything I was missing. After September 11, I felt intense guilt for not being home "where I belonged." I discovered that my need to be your pastor prevented the separation necessary to make the most of my renewal leave. Only when I completely let go of my professional identify did I realize how I was seeking to fulfill personal needs through ministry. That is not healthy for you or me. In the last month, I have finally been able to detach. In fact, I'm getting used to a more laid back life and discover I like it! I know you got along wonderfully without me. I still feel an intense call to pastoral ministry, however, and am eager to return to work.

I feel calm and centered now. I am stronger in body and spirit. I am well rested. I sense a peace and serenity that has often escaped me in the past. I know that I am loved and accepted for who I am. I realize that it is not what I do that is important. It's who I am. My prayer for the days ahead is that God might use me to be a spiritual leader at First Church, not as one who has arrived, but as a fellow traveler on the journey toward God in the company of Jesus Christ.

Being back in worship on Sunday was more wonderful than I ever imagined it would be. The hugs were even better! I have truly felt loved and sustained by your prayers. Thank you as well for your acts of kindness toward our family while I was gone. I have visited many churches over the past three months, but there wasn't even one which compares to the warmth, passion, caring and outward focus of First Church. I'm glad to be home.

The bell is ringing. Time to come in, Laurie! The big recess is over. But don't forget, you have to take time for recess every day. I'll see you tomorrow. Love, God.

Being and Doing

I have discovered new lands, God.

Losing sight of the shore for what seemed like a very long time,

Now I have returned whole.

I feel different.

I do not intend my life to ever be the same again.

Every day a precious gift.

But everyday is also a gift.

The ordinary, the mundane, the ho-hum.

May I be attentive to it all.

The stakes are high.

At stake is my physical, mental, emotional, relational and spiritual health.

At stake is the in-breaking of the kingdom of God.

Can I break the unhealthy patterns?

Can I end enslavement to the to-do list?

Can I leave behind the over-packed suitcase of my overcrowded life?

The bread of life and the cup of salvation given for you and for me.

Fill all of me with all of you.

Let me be—a pure expression of your love.

All you want is for me to love you.

I love you, God.

Playing at Christmas.

CHAPTER 14

Epilogue

THIRTEEN YEARS HAVE passed since my recess, but my renewal leave still seems like yesterday. Hardly a day goes by that I don't remember the joy of having three months away from my "life." Even though I had the good fortune to receive a Lilly Endowment grant that enabled me to do some traveling, the benefits I reaped are available to anyone who is able to have time away.

To devote 100 percent of my time and energy to nurturing my own soul and relationship with God was not only a privilege, it was essential to my spiritual, emotional and physical health. My renewal leave was not only a defining point in my ministry, it was the beginning of a sacred dance that saved my life.

Now, I am no longer at mid-career. It's more like three-quarters. Never could I have imagined where my professional career would take me over the past 13 years. But the details of my ministry are not nearly as important as a deeper awareness of the state of my heart and soul and my relationship with God. How has it gone, following up on my goals?

Seeking out times of worship when I have no leadership responsibilities. For six of the 13 years since my renewal leave I did not serve as a local church pastor but was a district superintendent in the West Michigan Conference of The United Methodist Church. I was blessed every Sunday by worshipping in the congregations for which I had supervisory responsibility. It was a refreshing break from the relentless grind of leading worship Sunday after Sunday.

I vow to set aside at least half an hour a day for Bible and spiritual reading, meditation, prayer and journal-keeping. The explosion of online resources over the past 13 years has enriched my personal devotional time. I have also come to the realization that I was not created to sit still to pray, so I make every effort to take a daily prayer walk—often in the late afternoon before evening meetings. I clear my mind of the clutter so that I can discover God in my surroundings. I attempt to see something new in God's creation each day.

I vow to find a spiritual guide with whom I will meet regularly. Two months after my renewal leave I found a spiritual director and have met with her once a month since then. I wouldn't have made it without her gentle reminder not to be too hard on myself, rest in God's grace and remain faithful to the call.

I vow to take more time for study and solitude. Since my leave I have taken a week every year for study and renewal. For the first five years I also spent 24 hours every month at a retreat center. Unfortunately, I was not able to sustain that spiritual discipline when I was a district superintendent. It's a growing edge.

I vow to become more detached from my work so that I can better serve my parishioners. Although I have a greater understanding of the spiritual and physical consequences of being a "quivering mass of availability," I still wrestle with work obsession in the second half of my career. It will likely always be my Achilles' heel.

I vow to become a better listener. Still wrestling with this.

I vow to give up control and allow the Spirit to master me. Ouch.

I vow to start a Taizé service at First Church. I began a monthly Taizé service at First United Methodist Church in Grand Rapids in September 2002, and it is still blessing members and guests alike.

I vow to find more opportunities to sing and play the organ. I will attend more concerts and plays. I pulled out my organ shoes to play in a yearly recital at First Church for a number of years after my leave, but those shoes have sat in a closet for the past two years.

I vow to get enough rest so that I am not continually exhausted. This last goal has been the most challenging because of my natural inclination to go and go and go. After 32 years of ministry, the work is still never done. Making wise decisions about the best use of my time in light of the mission of the congregation I serve as well as my own personal mission is at the cutting edge of my ministry.

The benefit of hindsight has revealed perhaps the greatest gift of my three-month recess, a gift that I was only able to clearly understand in the last five years. The single most powerful moment of my leave took place on a raw November Friday night in Taizé, France. It was just Jesus and me.

> When I kneel at the cross and place my forehead on the top of the vertical arm, I feel the power of Christ surge through me. It is one of the most incredible experiences of my life. As great big tears drop onto the floor, I remember the tears that Jesus shed in the Garden of Gethsemane. He felt everything that I feel. Although he was innocent, he took it all on himself.

I pray, "Lord Jesus, I give myself to you. I want to begin a new life now. I empty myself completely. I give to you all of my fears and failures. I release them into your hands. Fill all of me with all of you. Let me be a pure expression of your love. All you want is for me to love you. I love you, God."

Looking back, I realize that my leave unwittingly prepared me for the second half of my career and life, offering a more mature spiritual grounding to embrace personal and professional failure. Jesus was a suffering servant, who, by losing everything, even his life, saved us not for success but for giving ourselves away through service and sacrifice.

As I have grown older and, hopefully, wiser, I have realized that one of the greatest learnings of the Christian faith is that suffering is redemptive—that it is possible to descend into hell and rise again. Could it be that Jesus came to earth to show us how to suffer, how to carry "the legitimate pain of being human," as Carl Jung called it?

One day in each of our lives something will happen that we won't have the resources to handle or is beyond our control. We will experience the loss of relationships, dignity, health, jobs, dreams, trust and even hope. Things won't go our way, we will not get what we deserve and we will fall. We will be slandered, discounted and abandoned. This will happen more than once.

The suffering is beyond description. When Jesus told his disciples that he was going to undergo great suffering, Peter violently protested and Jesus said, "Get behind me. You are setting your mind not on divine things but on human things." Yet in the Garden of Gethsemane, even Jesus pleaded with God, "Father, if you are willing, remove this cup from me; yet, not my will but yours be done."

One of my friends has written, "Suffering is the launch pad for transformation." It's counter-intuitive, but our perceived failings can be the opportunity for spiritual growth and transformation. In the words of Franciscan priest Richard Rohr, falling down can really be falling upward. This is what distinguishes us as Christians. Experience is teaching me that fullness of life includes failure as well as success, falling down as well as getting up, and letting go as well as grabbing hold.

Wherever I serve, whether I succeed or fail or whether I live or die, I will follow the way of the cross, for I belong to God. So I am going to keep going out for recess. I am going to allow the enormity of God's grace to live in my heart through Jesus Christ so I can be a pure expression of God's love. I am going to grab hold of the ropes and swing as high and as low as I can. I will cherish every step of my journey with God. And that will be enough.

—Laurie Haller, 2014
www.lauriehaller.org

Taize service at First UMC, Grand Rapids.

Report to the Clergy in the West Michigan Annual Conference

JUNE 2002

Two years ago, after nearly 20 years of ministry, it became clear to me that I needed a break—a long break. I love being a pastor in a local church. I do not feel called to anything else. But I began to realize that the insistent demands of ministry were going to destroy my spirit if I continued along the same path. I was burned out.

I have always found it nearly impossible to keep boundaries between my personal and professional life. I find it very difficult to say no when there is a need in my church. The constant night meetings, the inability to keep my day off, emergencies at all times of the day and night, the choices of attending children's activities or fulfilling church obligations, the lack of sleep and the difficulty in practicing sabbath took their toll. I was terribly out of balance. I didn't know who I was anymore. I was too busy doing things for God that I forgot to spend time with God. The task of running a church became more important than my relationship with God.

Last fall I decided to take a three-month renewal leave from First Church in Grand Rapids, Michigan. I needed to get completely away with no family or church responsibilities. My congregation and my husband, Gary, gave me an incredible gift by encouraging me to go without feeling guilty.

I intentionally lived in solitude for most of my leave. My goal was to become reacquainted with myself and with God. I did not realize how hard and painful that process would be. I felt as if I had no identity. I had no one to take care of, nothing I had to do. It was just God and me.

I took an inventory of my life and learned a lot about myself during that time away. I realized that I wasn't happy. I admitted to myself that I was addicted to work. I discovered that many of the things I was doing in ministry were to fulfill my own needs, not the needs of those I am called to serve. I did not want the second half of my career to be like the first half.

As I received a clearer view of who I was, my spiritual struggles only intensified. Yet I felt God's presence in a way I never had before. It wasn't until the third month that I was able to empty myself completely. I arrived at the point where I did not need to be a pastor at First Church anymore. Nor did I need to go back into pastoral ministry. My identity was no longer dependent upon my being a pastor. First Church got along wonderfully well without me. I learned that I am not indispensable.

I came back to First Church last December rested, renewed, happy and, I believe, a little calmer, more centered and peace-filled. I set goals for myself and am working hard to ensure that my spiritual life remains vital. I now meet regularly with a spiritual director. I try to take time for sabbath every day. And I am more careful about saying yes. Of course, there are days when it all seems like a dream, especially during those inevitable busy weeks. But I know my experience was not a dream. I am different inside, and I don't intend to go back to the way it was before.

I know that my experience is not unique. Ministry is a difficult calling. The work is never done. We cannot please everyone. We feel isolated, discouraged to make friends in our congregations and having no time or energy to make friends outside of our congregations. There is often little connection or camaraderie among clergy.

We do not take care of ourselves very well, which is part of the reason for our healthcare struggles. Many insurance companies do not even want to quote on clergy health plans because clergy are too high a risk. It's not just the fact that we insure so many retirees. Clergy in general have a much higher use of mental health coverage than the average person. We are not as physically or emotionally healthy as we should be. It's time to become proactive in tending to our bodies, our minds and our spirits.

In the Gospel of Mark, Chapter 6, he writes: "The apostles gathered around Jesus and told him all that they had done and taught. He said to them, 'Come away to a deserted place all by yourselves and rest a while.' For many were coming and going, and they had no leisure even to eat. And they went away in the boat to a deserted place by themselves." If Jesus and his disciples needed to rest a while, I suspect we do as well.

I want to challenge each one of you this morning to think about how you can experience times of rest and renewal in the midst of ministry. Our *Book of Discipline* (2000) provides several ways for that to happen.

Paragraph 349.2 says: "A clergy member's continuing education and spiritual growth program should include such leaves at least one week each year and at least one month during one year of every quadrennium. Such leaves shall not be considered as part of the minister's vacations." Are you taking a week every year and a month every four years for spiritual formation? It's offered to us for a reason: We need spiritual renewal on a regular basis.

The *Book of Discipline* also provides for longer renewal leaves, such as the leave I took last year. Paragraph 349.3

says: "A clergy member may request a formational and spiritual growth leave of up to six months while continuing to hold an appointment in the local church. Such leaves are available to clergy members who have held full-time appointments for at least six years." You would receive your normal salary and benefits during your leave. If you have been a full-time pastor for six years, this kind of leave is offered to you. I would encourage you to think about it.

There is one more type of leave. Paragraph 350 allows clergy members to take a sabbatical leave for up to one year for a program of study or travel. This type of leave has to be approved by the Board of Ordained Ministry and the Clergy Session. In a sabbatical leave, you would not return to the same church after your leave but would receive a new appointment. Associate members or clergy members in full connection who have been serving in a full-time appointment for six consecutive years from the time of their reception into full or associate membership may be granted a sabbatical leave. The bishop would appoint you to sabbatical leave, and you would not receive a salary from a local church.

I can imagine what may be running through your minds right now. I never even knew this was available to me. My church would never let me leave for six or even three months. And even if they let me go, they need me. I can't be gone that long. Who would fill in for me? No one can replace me. If I were still receiving my salary, how would my replacement get paid? And how would I fund my leave if I want to do some traveling or continuing education?

Yes, the questions are real, and they are valid, but they are not insurmountable. There are several organizations that provide substantial grants for renewal leaves, most notably the Lilly Endowment. There are also funds available from our Board of Ordained Ministry.

I know that at times it seems more trouble than it's worth to take time away from active ministry. But I am convinced that the benefits far outweigh the excuses not to leave. By taking leaves, we prevent burn out. By stepping away from ministry for a time, we can better assess what we are doing, and we are better able to discern our call. We can go places or study things we don't have time to otherwise. We come back with renewed energy and vision.

We are not the only ones who benefit, however. Local churches discover they are not as dependent on the pastor as they think they are. Lay members are empowered to do ministry, which previously had only been done by the pastor. Most important, churches gain a better understanding of the unique stresses and challenges of pastoral ministry and are able to better support their pastors in the future.

The three-month leave I took last fall was a life-changing experience. I learned that central to effective ministry is the quality of my relationship with God. Keeping my soul alive is the most important activity in which I can engage as a pastor. Growing in my personal faith is not an option to which I can tend when everything else is done. It is essential to my calling.

Jesus said to his disciples, "Come away to a deserted place all by yourselves and rest a while."

I would encourage you to think about how you can most effectively tend to your soul.

—*Rev. Laurie Haller, Chair, Board of Ordained Ministry*

Snagging a rainbow trout.

About the Author

LAURIE HALLER IS
currently serving as senior
pastor of First United
Methodist Church in
Birmingham, Michigan. Laurie
grew up in southeastern
Pennsylvania as a Mennonite
and has degrees from
Wittenberg University, Yale
University School of Music
and Institute of Sacred Music
and Yale Divinity School.
She was a director of music
in a large United Methodist
Church in Connecticut before
becoming a pastor. Laurie was
among the first recipients of
a Lilly Endowment National
Clergy Renewal grant in 2000.
She has also served as the first
woman senior pastor at two of
the largest United Methodist
churches in Michigan.

Laurie has an intense curiosity about the world and its
people, a passion for spiritual leadership and a heart for
bringing in God's kingdom on this earth. You can find her
on the journey: serving, playing, running, singing, writing,
tending her spirit, keeping up with her three children and
grandson, advocating for the least of God's children and
leading from the heart. Laurie blogs at www.lauriehaller.org.

November 17, 2014

CPSIA information can be obtained
at www.ICGtesting.com
Printed in the USA
FSOW03n1337081016
25741FS